MW00613160

1. WORLD-RECORD TIGER SHARK, 1036 POUNDS

AN AMERICAN
ANGLER IN AUSTRALIA

by ZANE GREY

THE DERRYDALE PRESS
Lanham and New York

THE DERRYDALE PRESS

Published in the United States of America
by The Derrydale Press
A Member of the Rowman & Littlefield Publishing Group
4720 Boston Way, Lanham, Maryland 20706

Distributed by NATIONAL BOOK NETWORK, INC.

Copyright © 1937, 1965 by Zane Grey
First Derrydale paperback edition 2002
First Derrydale Blue Water Classics edition 2002

Library of Congress Control Number: 2001099112
ISBN 1-56416-204-4 (leatherbound : alk. paper)
ISBN 1-58667-087-5 (pbk. : alk. paper)

All rights reserved. No part of this publication may be reproduced,
stored in a retrieval system, or transmitted in any form or by any
means, electronic, mechanical, photocopying, recording, or otherwise,
without the prior permission of the publisher.

♾™ The paper used in this publication meets the minimum requirements of
American National Standard for Information Sciences—Permanence of
Paper for Printed Library Materials, ANSI/NISO Z39.48-1992.
Manufactured in the United States of America.

ILLUSTRATIONS

*The illustrations, grouped as a separate
section, will be found following p. 115*

[v]

Illustrations

AN AMERICAN ANGLER

IN AUSTRALIA

CHAPTER I

FOR A GOOD MANY YEARS I GRADUALLY YIELDED TO an impression that Australian waters, especially on the Indian Ocean side, would develop some of the greatest big-game fishing in the world.

At first, all I had to excite such interest were newspaper articles about man-eating sharks, and vague fish stories that drifted up from "down under." But in recent years I have corresponded with scientists, market fishermen, anglers, even missionaries, from all of whom I gathered data that added to my convictions, and finally sent me down to the under side of the world to see for myself, and prove, if possible, that my instinct and imagination were true guides. But though my chief concern was with Australia's thirteen thousand miles of rugged coast line, a small bit of which I hoped to explore, I was hardly prepared for this land of staggering contrasts, of unbelievable beasts, of the loveliest and strangest birds, of great modern English cities, of vast ranges that rivaled my beloved Arizona, and of endless forestland, or bush, as they call it, never yet adequately described, no doubt because of beauty and wildness beyond the power of any pen to delineate.

We arrived in Australia in time to welcome the New Year, 1936. I had seen many of the celebrated harbors of the world and was not prepared to surrender the supremacy of New York Harbor or that of San Francisco, not to mention Havana, Rio de Janeiro, and others, to this magnificent Australian refuge for ships with its shores of color and beauty. One of my camera men, Gus, exclaimed, enthusiastically and regretfully: "Say, this's got Frisco Harbor skinned to a frazzle." And I cannot do any better than quote this American slang.

Sydney is a great city, a real city, and there's no need to say more. During my short stay there I saw practically everything and was greatly impressed by many things. But this is to be an account of my fishing adventures in Australia, and it would take another volume to describe the country itself.

From what information I could gather, the neighborhood of Montague Island had yielded most of the swordfish that had been seen and caught by Australians. So after enjoying the hospitality of Sydney for several days, we gathered up bag and baggage and motored down the coast some two hundred and seventy-five miles to the little town of Bermagui, where we established our camp.

It seems, as the years go by, that every camp I pitch in places far from home grows more beautiful and romantic.

[2]

An American Angler in Australia

The setting of the one at Bermagui bore this out in the extreme. From the village a gradual ascent up a green wooded slope led to a jutting promontory that opened out above the sea. The bluff was bold and precipitous. A ragged rock-bound shoreline was never quiet. At all times I seemed aware of the insatiate crawling sea. The waves broke with a thundering crash and roar, and the swells roared to seething ruin upon the rocks. Looking north across a wide blue bay, we could see a long white beach. And behind it dense green forest, "bush," leading to a bold mountain range, and the dim calling purple of interior Australia. This shoreline swung far to the north, ending in a cape that extended out, pointing to Montague Island, bare and bleak, with its lighthouse standing erect, like a gray sentinel.

At this side of the promontory the great trees failed, leaving only a few standing away from the storm winds of the Antarctic, with bleached gnarled branches. Beyond lay a few logs and these led to a long green slope down to the sea.

Camp of a dozen or so of tents we located in a grove of widely-separated eucalyptus trees—gum trees they are called in Australia. They reminded me of the pohutukawa trees of New Zealand. There were sunny glades and plenty of shade, and foliage for the wind to sigh or mourn or roar through, according to the mood of the wind. The fragrance of these trees I had long known, because I have

[3]

eucalyptus on my place in California, some lovely, lofty, silver-barked trees, and others low and dense, bearing the scarlet flowers. But here the fragrance was penetrating and thick, like that of a fir forest in Oregon, only stronger. It pasted your nostrils shut.

Birds new to me sang in these trees and they were unnamable to me for a while, except the gulls, that come right into camp, up into the woods. This was unprecedented and very intriguing. Sea birds, fish-eaters, visiting me in camp! It was a good augury. Maybe they thought I would bring lots of fish meat for them to eat.

And the kookaburra, the laughing jackass, what shall I say of this laughing devil of a friendly ludicrous bird? They came early and late, they sat and watched me, turning their heads, as if to express their interest, if not resentment: "Now who is this fellow, anyhow? We'll have to see about him."

They were quite large, rather bulky forward, with dull white breasts and gray backs and markings, with big heads and wicked long bills. All about them comic and friendly, except that terrible laugh! It awakened me at dawn, and I heard it after I went to bed. I knew I would love them, despite the fear that maybe they were "giving me the laugh," and pealing out with "Haw! Haw! Haw!" in several raucous tones at my temerity and audacity in coming nine thousand miles to catch some fish. That laugh

[4]

discouraged me a little. But as far as the fish were concerned I had only to look out over that dark blue ocean, the Tasman Sea, notorious for its currents and storms, its schools of whales and fish, to know that I would find new and boundless sport.

CHAPTER II

THE ELEMENT OF FAMILIARITY IN ALL THIS newness and strangeness of Australia was supplied by the presence of my boatman, Peter Williams, of New Zealand, and my launch, the *Avalon*. She had been constructed from my design by Collings in Auckland, and is comfortable, fast, and seaworthy. With a long hard fishing trip planned, it is imperative that these features be present.

Peter used to be a whaler and that is why he is so efficient with ropes and moorings and boats. He is the brawniest and best man with a gaff who has ever stood beside me. Since 1927, when I first visited New Zealand, he has fished with me in many waters besides his own— California, Mexican coast, Galapagos, Tahiti, South Sea Islands, and now we are in Australia. It is needless to say that we look for an outstanding and wonderful experience.

From talking with the native fishermen and market fishermen at Bermagui, I learned considerable from which I could make deductions. There were a number of conflicting opinions, as well as some general statements in which all concurred. One was that I could hardly be expected to catch a swordfish before February. And this was mid-January.

The old familiar wind and rough seas marked the first few days at Bermagui. But we could not have gone out in any event, as it is a big job to pitch a camp of a dozen tents, all on board floors, and to build a serviceable kitchen and dining-room. The way we camp puts us in conflict with the elements, if not wholly at their mercy. But that is what I love about living in the open—rain, shine, wind, calm, gale, and torrential downpour. We have already had them all.

On January 11th we started out for our first run, really a scouting trip. For me it was difficult and poignant to take the initial step. That is because I *know* what this start entails—the beginning of a protracted period of hazardous, nerve-wracking, toilsome days. To get results you have to run out every day that is possible, and as the old Scotchman said, "If you want to cetch fish you must keep your flea in the water." If you substitute the word bait for "flea" you will have a slogan for successful salt-water fishing.

We ran from our mooring out the mouth of a little river, against an incoming tide, with a rugged low headland of rock on our right and a curved sand spit on our left, into a wide bay. A long white beach wandered away

[7]

to the north, and dim in the distance was our objective, Montague Island. Gulls were absent, at least on the water, and there was no evidence of bait or fish. The day was overcast, with promise of clearing.

Peter called our camera-boat the Tin Horn. Its name was really *Tin Hare*, but it pleased his sense of humor to call it Tin Horn. She was long and well built, and appeared to be a most satisfactory vessel for taking pictures. I would not have fished out of her under any circumstances, because the cockpit was too far back, and therefore the fishing-chairs too far from the stern. You would have to fight a fish from either side; and when a swordfish ran under the boat, which is a likely occurrence, it would be just too bad. Australian anglers, after the manner of New Zealanders, run their boats while they are fast to a fish, usually in the direction the fish is going, and less often away from him. My method is to stop a fish after the first hard run, and fight him.

My camera crew, Bowen, Anderson, and Morhardt, experienced and clever as they are in photography, were utter novices in big-game sea-angling. The Warren Brothers, Ike and Bill, market fishermen and good fellows hired as crew of the *Tin Hare*, had no understanding of our methods. I felt a grim amusement when I realized what the *Tin Hare* was in for; and also a keen relish in prospect of fun and sport and disaster and hazard on board the boat. Such things always promise the

incidents that make for good stories. Bowen had con-
scripted or shanghaied his pretty wife, Marge, for script
girl; and I certainly felt concern for her.

We put out the teasers and Peter handed me a rod:
"All set, sir," he said. "Might as well troll to and fro,
going to that island. We'll pick up a big fish some day."

Peter and I had the same reactions to fishing, except in
extraordinary cases. I sustained an old familiar tingling
as I settled down into the fishing-chair, rested the rod on
the gunwale, took the line in my hand, and set my eyes
upon the bait. It was a mullet and small. Now mullet
are indeed tidbits for all kinds of big sea fish, but they
do not troll well.

It is impossible to watch a bait *all the time*. Nevertheless, you must almost do that if you expect to see a Marlin
or a mako or a broadbill flash up out of the depths. If
you see him first you have the advantage. I have often
wondered how many fish I fail to see, as they go by.
Many and many a one, I know. It is a mistake to imagine
that even half of the fish you raise come for the bait, and
it takes years of practice to discern them, except those
that come close or strike. Raising a fish means drawing
it up from the depths somewhere by the use of teasers.

I took a quick glance at bait and teasers and then at the
long winding white shoreline, the dark range of mountains, the sea all around, and then my eyes returned. This
is a continual process. A good angler should see every-

thing, which is impossible. But particularly he must not miss fins on the surface, dim shapes of gray or green or purple in the swells, birds and their actions, and splashes of fish near or far.

The water of this Australian sea is dark in color, darker, I think, than that of New Zealand, though this seems unreasonable. Flash of the weaving teasers would not show one-tenth so far as in the crystal waters of the South Seas. Fish here could not possibly have the range of vision that they have in tropic seas. We had to find out what teasers worked best and how to manipulate them.

It took two hours to run out to Montague Island, but the time seemed short. Islands always fascinate me. How many lonely lighthouses have I seen! Somehow this one reminded me of Alacrans in the Caribbean Sea. That one was so lonely, so seldom visited, that more than one lighthouse-keeper had gone insane. Montague is a barren rock rising like a hump-backed whale. Tufts of green-yellow grass seem its sole vegetation. But for the most part bare rocks rounded by wind and sea led the gaze to the tower standing on the summit, apprehensively facing the sea. There was an attraction about Montague which I may define later.

For bait we caught small kingfish, or yellowtail, *Cereola dorsalis,* which is the proper name, and a small mackeral which the boatman called bonito. This species looked more like a skipjack; a bonito has fewer stripes. It was a pretty, shiny fish.

We trolled bait of this kind around the island and then ran out a mile or more. Gulls were few and far between. I sighted one shark fin cutting the water. Outside we ran upon the *Tin Hare* performing some remarkable evolutions. Emil (Morhardt) had hooked a hammerhead shark and was having his troubles. The shark was heavy and Emil had forgotten to put on the harness. This fact, coupled with the movements of the boat, made him a rather helpless, ludicrous picture. But he was enraptured. In fact they were all excited. They yelled at us, "Whoopee! We've got one on!"

I hung around them for a while, watching, and resisting my strong desire to yell, "Stop the boat and fight the fish!"

Presently we raised a hammerhead. This species of shark is probably nearly the same in all waters. But this one had a lighter and more curved dorsal fin, and the way it cut the water, as the big fish came weaving and dashing after us, was something worth photographing. A hammerhead has poor eyesight. He trails his prey by scent, and his peculiar weaving pursuit is wholly due to that. The most remarkable feature about the hammerhead, *Squalus zygaena,* is the long hammer-like head, on the extreme front of which runs a deep little groove leading to the nostrils at each end. This has been developed to catch more scent in the water. His eyes are also located at each end.

We enticed this fellow to follow the bait. When a second and larger one appeared I had to draw the bait in to keep him from getting it. The savagery of the sea is exemplified in the fierce, swift action of sharks. I hate sharks, and have killed a thousand, and have an inkling that I'll add another thousand to my list here.

We ran over to watch Emil, who in the meantime had conquered his hammerhead. They hauled it on board. Soon after that we headed back toward Bermagui. I noticed birds working in shore, and running over we found shearwater ducks (mutton birds) and gannet working in a tide-rip where patches of bait showed. A big commotion a mile away looked like a swordfish splash, so we ran down. I often raise and catch swordfish that I sight at a distance. We could not locate this one, however, though we kept trolling around.

Presently the other boat flagged us, and we ran over to find that they had seen an enormous black Marlin rolling around in a patch of bait. We trolled there for an hour without results. Both the Warrens and my men claimed this Marlin was huge, fully sixteen feet long. At least it was the largest these market fishermen had seen.

There was nothing more that happened that day, except a silver pall of rain shrouding the mountains. I called it a good day.

There is always the next day to lure with its possibilities. No two days are alike. The following morning we were out bright and early, trolling the baits we had left from the preceding trip. Hungry swordfish will take anything, but you need a live bait for some of them. Fish that are not hungry at all will rise to follow the teasers, sometimes for miles. These are the aggravating ones. But I have so often teased and provoked one to strike that I generally work with them till they go away.

A big long swell was running, the kind upon which you don't want the wind to work further. It was clear and sunny, though in the southeast there loomed a cloud I did not like. I had an idea the wind would come, but straightway forgot it.

Four miles out I sighted a long sickle fin cutting through a swell. Did I yell, "Marlin!"? I certainly did. An instant later Peter sighted another farther out, and this tail fin belonged to a large fish. I could not tell whether or not it indicated a black Marlin. It stood up three feet or more, and that much would make a tail spread of over six feet. These Marlin were riding the swells and they were moving fast. The tails would come up out of the top of a swell and cut the water at more than a ten-knot speed. Then they would vanish. It is always necessary to run the boat in the right direction to head the fish off. The *Avalon* is fast—she can do eighteen knots when opened up—but we could not catch up with the big fellow.

We did, however, show a bait to the smaller Marlin. He saw it flash from over a hundred feet distant. When he swirled with that unmistakable flip of his tail I yelled: "He's coming, boys. Look out!"

And I'd hardly uttered the words when there he was shooting like a huge purple bird for my bait. I let go my line even before he reached it, and then as the reel whizzed I pressed my gloved hand down to prevent an overrun. You handle every strike of a Marlin differently. In this case I did what would be right in most cases. When he felt the hook he came out, a long, lean fish of some three hundred pounds, and he threw that bait thirty feet. From the feel of the action I judged the hook had caught on his long jaw and did not penetrate. I have caught Marlin, though, with only the point of the hook in the bone, not in to the barb. Peter gave vent to some thoroughly American language, which he had learned from me and which would not look so well in print.

"Only an incident of the day, Pete, old top," I said. "Put on another bait."

"But it's the *first* day, sir," he expostulated. Peter and my other men wanted me to make the first catch for 1936.

We ran on. I trolled that bait clean to Montague Island. There were birds to the eastward, and I gave that stretch a going over. Six of them were albatross. This was my very first time to fish right with these falcons of the sea, and I watched them till they sailed away.

Next day there were three other boats already at Montague. One of these passed us and kindly threw us a yellowtail bait, but it fell short into the water. Off the north end of the island, after some time trolling, we managed to catch a few bait. And we were scarcely two hundred feet from the rocks when we put these smaller fish on and started to troll.

We had not passed the corner of the island when I saw a blue flash and a ragged fin coming from the left. It was a Marlin and he took my bait with a rush. At the same time I saw a sharp bill back of Gus's hook. I shouted: "Look out! There's another!" This one got Gus's bait and he pulled it off for the simple reason that Gus was so scared or excited that he held on to the line with grim tenacity. I made a remark. Gus said: "Was that your fish?"

"No, it wasn't," I replied. "The idea is when you have a fish rush your bait to let him have it."

"Where's your—fish?" gasped Gus.

"He doesn't want to stop going places, so I'll have to stop him."

I hooked the Marlin, and he leaped splendidly, fully six hundred feet away and close to the camera boat.

The surprised crew and picture men, who didn't know what was happening, nearly fell overboard. But they soon got busy. Bowen appeared to be frantic because the Warrens were reluctant to run their boat at the fish. They were right, of course. A second boat has no business near another one in which an angler has hooked a fish. But Bowen's idea was to shoot motion pictures. He did not care if they did risk cutting my line.

What with the jumping antics of the Marlin and the attempts of the *Tin Hare* to get on top of it we had lots of fun for a little while. I made rather short work of that Marlin, because I discovered I, too, wanted the credit of the first one for 1936. We soon had him on board. Peter beamed and congratulated me. He also waved the Marlin flag at the other boat.

Baiting up again, we ran out. Gus had photographed some of the leaps of this fish, and he was happy, too. Presently I saw a Marlin slide out and shake himself, perhaps half a mile out. I pointed. Peter said he had seen the splash. He did not need to be told to hook the *Avalon* up and speed in the direction I had pointed.

"Shut her off, Peter," I called, and stood up. "Work around here."

Presently I saw the purple form of a Marlin looming up, and my old familiar cry pealed out, "There he is!" I have probably called that out thousands of times.

This fish came directly to the bait. But he did not take it at once, as I expected. He weaved to and fro. He rushed it, came up alongside it, struck at it. "Son of a gun is leary," I said.

"He'll take it," replied Peter, and sure enough he did. But he let it go. And though he came back, time and again, he would not strike. No doubt he thought there was something wrong about that bait and he was not hungry enough to be unwary. When Marlin are hungry they will strike; when they are ravenous they will stick their heads out of the water back of the boat to take a bait.

In the next three hours I raised several more Marlin off the point of the island, but they had evidently fed and would not take. The other boat raised one, and then Bowen was too slow in pulling his bait away from a hammerhead. It got the bait and the hook. Evidently this made Bowen angry, for he began to jerk and haul strenuously. His drag was too strong. I feared the shark would pull him overboard. The rod wagged to and fro, and then suddenly, when the shark pulled free of the hook, Bowen went over backwards, clean out of the chair.

Soon after that I sunk my bait to a gray shadow, and soon was fast to some kind of a shark. I worked hard on it, for practice more than anything else, and soon had it up.

"Darned old rearimi!" ejaculated Peter. But Pat, the market fisherman on our boat, said it was a gray pointer. Anyway, Peter gaffed it, and the two of them held the shark for a splashing mêlée while the camera boat stood by. I heard Bowen yell through his megaphone, "Roll 'em along!" And in Hollywood parlance that meant to start the electric motors on the motion-picture cameras.

After that fun we caught another bait. I noticed that the sea was rising outside and I thought we had better start back to Bermagui. Still I lingered to try for some more. Presently Gus hooked a good-sized bonito.

We were close to the rocks where the herd of sea lions held forth. Half a dozen big bulls dived off and made for the fish. I jerked the rod out of Gus's hand. But hard as I pumped and wound I could not get that bonito away from them.

Then the camera crew went wild. It had not occurred to me till then just what an unusual picture that action would make. But with seals fighting over my bait, leaping out, darting to and fro, I soon realized the fact. So instead of trying to get my bait in I left it out there and jerked it this way and that to excite the seals further. This worked. The sea lions made such a commotion that others piled off the rocks until the sea appeared alive with graceful brown forms on the surface and under.

Then what I might have suspected actually happened. I hooked a big bull sea lion in the chin, and he did not like that at all. In fact he made a vociferous and violent protest. He stood half his massive body high out of the water and tussled like a huge dog. He jerked his head from side to side, while the bait dangled about for the other sea lions to snatch it.

Here I was hooked to a six-hundred-pound sea lion, on a bait tackle! I did not want to kill the beast or leave the hook, leader, and part of the line hanging from his jaw. We had to follow the beast to keep him from running off more line. I was in a quandary. Peter was wrathful. "Haul the plugger up here. I'll gaff him!"

"Haul him up? Ha! Ha! I see myself. He's as strong as an elephant." But Bowen and his crew had a different point of view. Theirs was a picture angle. And they made the best of it. Finally I told Peter to run close to the sea lion and try to cut the leader. I held the brute as hard as I could, with a feeling something was going to break. Peter managed, however, to get hold of the wire, and then the hook pulled out, to the chagrin of our camera men.

It occurred to me then that the incident had been unique and remarkable. I have hooked many denizens of the deep, like dolphin, rays, devilfish, sawfish, octopus, and now finally a big sea lion.

"Pete, what do you know about that?" I exclaimed. "Something new!"

"Right-o, sir. I've a hunch we might hook anything in these unfished waters."

That was a thrilling thought and I heartily accepted it.

CHAPTER III

AT MIDNIGHT THE WIND IN THE TREE TOPS awakened me. It had a low, menacing sound. I got up and went out on the bluff, and I was more than rewarded.

Beneath me the great rollers crashed to ruin on the rocks, with incessant changing roar. A half-moon, low down, cast a pale light upon the sea. Overhead Orion appeared as always, sloping to the west. And the Southern Cross, that magnificent and compelling constellation, blazed with white fire, high in the heavens. Far out to sea there were gloom and mystery.

At once I grasped a difference between this scene and any other I had come upon. I sensed a far country, a country surrounded by a vast ocean, with something hanging over it that must have been the influence of the Antarctic. Yet despite the brooding mood, the aloofness, almost a forbidding dark brightness, like the light which comes sometimes before a storm breaks at sunset, the scene was beautiful and unforgettable. And I fell under its spell.

An American Angler in Australia

At five the next morning there was a sunrise remarkable in the extreme. A dark mass of cloud overhung the east. Beneath it a broad band of clear sky turned gradually gold, until the blazing disc of the sun tipped the horizon line, and then there came a transfiguration of sea, sky, and cloud. For a few moments there was a glorious light too dazzling for the gaze of man. One thing a fisherman sees far more than his fellow men, and that is the coming of the dawn and the breaking of the light, and the bursting of the sun into its supremacy.

Here at Bermagui the early morning never fails to reward the appreciative watcher. The birds at the first gray change from the darkness—the kookaburras first, with their strange, incorrigible, humorous laughter, wild, startling, concatenated; then the other birds, the gulls walking with dignity right into camp, and the wrens and robins and magpies. I miss the bell birds and the tuis of New Zealand, than which no other birds of far countries have more intrigued me.

After several days of wind and rain and stormy sea there came a spell of fine weather. It was as welcome as May flowers. It gave me a chance to run out to sea, to fish hard every day, to get my bearings on this foreign shore.

I caught six Marlin swordfish between 250 and 300 pounds in weight, and raised or sighted about thirty. This during a period of a week and a half, with only one windy day, was a very agreeable surprise, and augured well for big results later. The crew of the *Tin Horn* accounted for three fish, two hammerheads, and one mako. Sight of this latter shark satisfactorily identified this species in Australian waters.

I lost two really fine fish, the larger of which was a mako of about 600 pounds. I had no idea that the strike came from a mako until I hooked him. Then he ran and leaped. One flashing sight of a great white-and-blue, huge-finned fish high in the air was enough to make Peter and me yell wildly in unison. We rejoiced to see one of our old shark friends, or enemies, at the end of my line. He fell back with a crash and sent a great splash skyward. Then to further convince us of his kinship with the makos he swam up to the boat, to see what it was all about. His coal-black eye, staring and cruel, his pointed nose, his savage underhung jaw, partly open to disclose great curved fangs, his round body, potent with tremendous power, his utter lack of fear of man or boat—these identified him as the *mako-mako*, first named by Polynesians in the South Seas, and in New Zealand by the Maoris. The Australian name for this species is bluepointer. I have no doubt but that this provincial name will give way to the better and correct "mako."

I was holding him hard and Peter was speculating whether or not to attempt to gaff him, when he cut my leader off as neatly as if he had used steel shears.

An American Angler in Australia

The wire sang as it flipped back to us. A Marlin leader is really not good to use on mako, though I have caught many on it. I prefer specially-made leaders of heavy wire and big hooks for this powerful and savage-biting shark.

The other fish I lost was a striped Marlin that would have weighed more than four hundred pounds. But I never caught him to find out. While trolling I always wear gloves. In hooking fish and fighting them I find gloves indispensable. But they get hot at times and uncomfortable. This day I removed them for a moment—and then, of course, it happened. A big purple-banded Marlin shot up as swiftly as a meteor. He took the bait and was off. I had to press both my ungloved hands down on the whizzing reel of line to prevent an overrun and backlash. I burned my hands. But I could not let go to set the drag. The fish leaped into the air, a beautiful bronze-and-silver Marlin, barred with broad blue bands, one of the largest of his kind; and with a swing of his savage head he flung bait and hook back at us. That was a disappointment, of course, but as I had a fish on the stern I managed to survive the loss.

Bait we found difficult to procure. The yellowtail and bonito around Montague Island had a most unobliging habit of biting not more than about once a week. The native boatmen on the *Tin Horn* promised to catch salmon for us, but up to the date of this writing they did not do so. I found myself longing for the huge schools of trevalli and kahawai that make fishing in New Zealand such a joy. The fishing along this Australian coast is too new and strange and uncertain for me to make any predictions as yet.

My first really big fish I raised opposite the lighthouse on Montague, not very far out. He struck at the bait. missed it, and left a frothy boil on the water. Then he came back at it, a dark shape, incredibly swift, and actually took it without showing his spear. He was off as fast as the big Marlin I lost. When I hooked him I came up solid on a heavy fish. The sensation was most agreeable, although the jerk shifted me off my chair and almost cracked my neck.

We signaled the camera-boat to speed up. My line was reeling off and beginning to surface. Peter yelled that he was coming up. This moment of expectation is always thrilling. He broke water, showing a short black bill, a big head and deep body, shining like a black opal.

"Black Marlin!" I whooped, and Peter echoed me.

After a moment I warned Peter to steady up and keep away from him, and to wave back the keen camera men, who would have run right on top of the fish. Then I "put the wood on him," as the American angling saying goes. We got within two hundred feet, and signaled the camera-boat to come along behind and somewhat out to the right. In that position we ran along with the black Marlin—because I could not stop him at that stage—until I saw the line rising to the surface, indication that he was about to jump.

I was all excitement, yet tense with caution and strong physical exertion. He was hard to hold. His blunt bill appeared splitting the surface, and then his head, his broad shoulders, his purple back, and all of him wagged up and out, until he cleared the water by several feet. His back was toward me, but it was easy to estimate his size and I let out a second whoop. I heard the crew of the *Tin Horn* screaming like lunatics. They had never seen a fish approaching the size and beauty of this one.

He plunged back with a thundering smash. Then, as I expected, he came out again, faster, this time broadside, and indeed a wonderful picture for an angler to gloat over.

"Oh, gosh!" I groaned. "If the camera boys only get that one in their little black box!"

His third leap was still faster, and more of a spectacle, as he went low and long, all of him up, with his wide tail waving. This time he dived back and sounded. He went deep and stayed down.

I fought him an hour or more before I could hold him even a little. Following that, he rose again to the surface, to repeat his trio of leaps, and after that he woke up and tore the sea to shreds. He made his most magnificent leap, which I could not see, in front of the boat. Gus was up there on the boat, and when he came back to the cockpit he was beside himself with triumph and ecstasy.

"Holy Mackali! what a fish! I had him in the finder every jump."

When the black Marlin soused back the last time I had a feeling we would see no more of him until I brought him up to gaff. I was right, and this time did not arrive for over and hour. We were extremely careful at this most hazardous moment, and as luck would have it Peter soon had a rope round the Marlin's tail. And I knew I had the record swordfish for Australia.

We steamed back to Bermagui and the men carried the black Marlin ashore. Lying on the green grass, the fish looked grand. He was indeed a black opal hue. When I named this species some ten years ago I should have used the word opal and have called it black opal Marlin. That would have been especially felicitous for Australia. He was a short fish, broad and deep and round, and I estimated his weight as five hundred pounds. But I missed it. The scales we procured at a Bermagui store were inadequate, weighing only in periods of ten. Peter called out: "Four hundred eighty. Let it go at that."

"Not on your life, Pete," I protested. "Don't you see the scale point wavers beyond 480. He weighs something beyond 480." And I stuck to that—some unknown pounds beyond 480.

There was a big crowd of spectators to see that weighing of Bermagui's biggest swordfish so far, and it reminded me of the times at Avalon, when thousands of people would flock out to see a broadbill I had brought in.

Next day the ocean around Montague Island was empty for me. My boat could not raise a fish of any kind. But other boats had better luck. I saw one flag flying and another boat manifestly fighting a fish.

About three o'clock we started the long run back to Bermagui. The sea had whipped up a little, and it promised to get rough. The *Tin Horn* had a lead of a couple of miles on us. We got about that distance from the island and had caught up somewhat with my camera-boat when I saw that some one had hooked a fish. We ran ahead full speed, and soon drew within range to see what was going on.

Bowen had the rod and it was evident that whatever was on the rod had Bowen. He was sturdy and strong, the same as Emil, but he had never caught a swordfish, and to catch a big one off that boat, with the Warrens running it, would be little short of a miracle. The fish came up to surf-board along the waves, making the water fly in sheets. I had a poor glimpse of it. But Peter said, "Black Marlin, and a good fish, too!"

The next hour and more was harder on me that on Ed Bowen, I was sure. But I hung around, camera in hand, hoping the fish would broach. However, he did not come up; he worked out to sea. Strenuously as Ed pumped and wound, he got line in only when the boatman ran up on the fish. They ran in circles. They halted when the fish was running and went on when he was momentarily stopped. From the way Ed's rod wagged, I judged the fish to be pretty heavy. Peter said not so big. He grew tired of circling their boat endlessly and wanted to turn back for Bermagui. I stayed as long as I could stand it. I wanted to tell Ed and those boatmen *what to do*. But if I *had* told them, and then they lost the fish, they would have blamed me—a terrible thing, as I knew to my cost. Finally I took up a megaphone and called Ed, "Hey there—that fish is as tired as he'll ever get."

"Tired?—Good Lord!—I'm the tired one!" panted Ed. "What'll I do?"

"Stop the boat and fight him."

"Hell! He won't stop—neither will these boatmen."

"Try it once."

They made a valiant effort. Ed heaved and wound mightily. He yelled at me, "Notify Australian Government—I'm pulling up—another island for them!"

"Aw, you're not pulling anything. That fish doesn't know he's hooked."

"Go AWAY!" bawled Ed. "Wanna make me—lose him?"

Peter interposed with an encouraging shout: "You'll get him. Take it slower. Just keep a good strain on him. You'll get him."

"That's telling me," Ed yelled back, gratefully.

We left them to their fate and ran back to Bermagui, arriving about five o'clock.

Just before dark the *Tin Horn* steamed in, proudly flying a flag. They had their fish. It was a good one, as Pete had said, and weighed four hundred pounds. I congratulated Ed on a really remarkable feat. He beamed. "My back's broke. Three hours! I never worked so hard in all my life."

And then he burst into a marvelous narrative of what had happened on board the *Tin Horn*. It differed vastly from the story the boatmen told. Emil, who is a temperamental artist, had still a weirder story to tell. But for me each and every word was significant with proof of the humor, the sport, the thrill, the misery and ecstasy of big-game fishing.

CHAPTER IV

TACKLE AND METHOD IN ANGLING ARE THINGS very important to fishermen. And they cause more argument, controversies, and, alas! more ill-will than anything in the big-game fishing, unless it is the competition and rivalry that seem unfortunately inseparable from the sport.

There was a time when I used to tell anglers what I believed to be the proper and best way to fish. I never do that any more, unless directly asked by some sincere amateur. But all fishermen are interested in what the others use, and here in Australia I find myself vastly intrigued and confounded by the "gear" these fishermen have and the way they use it. To give them just credit, I am bound to admit that they have done remarkably well with wrong measures.

I have not seen any angler using the drifting method of fishing in Australian waters. This is the one mostly used in New Zealand. It remains to be seen how good or bad it will be here. Here they troll from early till late, and in our American fishing parlance, they run the wheels off the boat. I admit that and will say that these gentlemen have started right.

There is no limit to these fishing-waters. Swordfish are here, there, and everywhere. In deep waters I do not believe they can be located daily at any given point out at sea. Around the islands and near shore they can be depended on to come in every few days. So far during my six weeks' fishing here I find the Marlin ravenously hungry. This makes a vast difference. Anybody can hook a hungry fish. Which explains the incredible success some methods attain. It can be explained by realizing that a hungry swordfish could be hooked with a flatiron or cricket bat. Catching it, and repeating, of course, are a different matter.

Fishing at Bermagui, Narooma and Eden, on this South Coast, is only three years old. The first method, and one still in use here, was to troll with a heavy lead on the line. It was attached to the leader by a ring from which a string stretched up to the boat. In the event of a strike the lead could be jerked free from the leader.

Another method, and one still more advocated at this date, is to troll the bait back a hundred and fifty feet or more, with a lighter lead. The revolving bait is considered a desirable feature. In this style the teasers also were dragged quite far back.

Modifications and variations of these methods are numerous.

An American Angler in Australia

To catch fish is not all of fishing, to be sure, and any device or method is permissible so long as it pleases an angler and lends to his sport that personal and peculiar fetish which is one of the joys of the game. I doubt that there ever was a fisherman who did not conceive and invent some gadget all his own, and some manner of using it that to him was the best. That is one of the many reasons why fishing, to my way of thinking, is the greatest of all sports.

The possibilities of Australian big-game fishing intrigue me and excite me more and more, as I fish myself, and receive more and more word from different and widely separated places on Australia's grand coast of thirteen thousand miles.

I expected to find Australia and New Zealand somewhat alike, and the fishing also. They are totally different. In any fishing trip, such as I call worthy of the name, there are many considerations that make for the ultimate success and memorable record. The beauty and color of the surrounding country, the birds and snakes and animals, the trees and hills, the long sandy beaches, and the desolate ragged shorelines, the lonely islands—all these and many more appeal to me as much as the actual roaming the sea, in rain and shine, in calm and storm, and the catching of great game fish.

One of the pleasantest experiences I have ever had, and one the joy of which will grow in memory, is to be awakened in the dusk of dawn by the kookaburras. That is unique. The big mollyhawks of New Zealand, the laughing gulls of California, that awaken you at dawn and are things never forgotten, cannot compare with these strange and homely and humorous jackasses of the Australian woods.

We ran our score of big fish caught up to twenty-one in seven weeks, which list, considering that half this time was too bad weather to fish, and that it included my black Marlin record of four hundred and eighty pounds, two of the same around four hundred pounds, and a really rare fish, the green Fox thresher, must be considered very good indeed.

It turned out, however, that my last day off Bermagui was really the most thrilling and profitable to Australia, as well as to me.

This was an unusually beautiful day for any sea. The morning was sunny, warm, and still. There seemed to be the balminess of spring in the air. We got an early start, a little after sunrise, with the idea of running far offshore —"out wide," the market fishermen call it—into the equatorial stream.

I had been out in this current several times off Montague Island, but not very far, and not to study it particularly. The camera crew came on the *Avalon* with me, owing to their boat being in need of engine repairs.

Bait was easy to catch and quite abundant, which fact

always lends an auspicious start to a fish day. The boys yelled in competition as they hauled in the yellowtail (king fish), bonito, and salmon. Shearwater ducks were wheeling over the schools of bait, and the gannets were making their magnificent dives from aloft. A gannet, by the way, is the grandest of all sea-fowl divers.

Mr. Rogers had been among the Marlin the day before, fifteen miles northeast of Montague, and Mr. Lynn had also been among them twenty miles directly east of Bermagui. Our plan was to locate one or other of them, and find the fish. As a matter of fact, we ran seventy miles that day and could not even get sight of them. But we found the fish and they did not. This lent additional substantiation to my theory that in a fast-moving clean current, fish will never be found in the same place the next day. It is useless to take marks on the mountains for the purpose of locating a place out at sea where the fish were found today, because they go with the current and the bait. In deep water, say two hundred and twenty-five fathoms off Bermagui, the bottom has no influence whatever on the fish. In shallow water the bottom has really great influence.

We ran thirty miles by noon. No fish sign of any kind —no birds or bait or splashes or fins—just one vast heaving waste of lonely sea, like a shimmering opal.

After lunch I told the outfit that I guessed it was up to me to find some kind of fish, so I climbed forward and stood at the mast to scan the sea. This was an old familiar, thrilling custom of mine, and had been learned over many years roaming the sea for signs of tuna or broadbill swordfish. In the former case you see splashes or dark patches on the glassy sea; in the latter you see the great sickle fins of that old gladiator *Xiphias gladius*, surely the most wonderful spectacle for a sea angler.

In this case, however, all I sighted was a hammerhead shark. His sharp oval fin looked pretty large, and as his acquisition might tend to good fortune, I decided to drop him a bait and incidentally show my camera crew, who had been complaining of hard battles with sharks, how easy it could be done.

Using a leader with a small hook, I had the boatman put on a small piece of bait, and crossed the track of the hammerhead with it. When he struck the scent in the water he went wild, and came rushing up the wake, his big black fin weaving to and fro, until he struck. Hammerheads have rather small mouths, but they are easily hooked by this method. In a couple of minutes I had hold of this fellow.

After hooking him I was careful not to *pull hard* on him. That is the secret of my method with sharks, of which I have caught a thousand. They are all alike. They *hate* the pull of a line and will react violently, according to what pressure is brought to bear. If they are not "horsed," as the saying goes, they can be led up to the boat to the gaff. This means a lot of strenuous exercise for the boatmen, but only adds to the fun. Shooting, as is employed here in Australia, and harpooning, as done in New Zealand, disqualify a fish.

I had this hammerhead up to the boat in twelve minutes, and I never heaved hard on him once. Emil, my still photographer, a big strong fellow, had had a three-hour battle with one a little smaller, and he simply marveled at the trick I had played on the shark, and him, too.

There was a merry splashing mêlée at the gaffing of this hammerhead, in which all the outfit engaged. It was the largest hammerhead I had seen in Australian waters, probably close to six hundred pounds. Off the Perlos Islands I have seen eighteen-foot hammerheads, with heads a third that wide. I understand the Great Barrier Reef has twenty-two-foot hammerheads. Australia is verily the land, or water, for sharks; and I am vastly curious to see what a big one will do to me. Mr. Bullen was four and a half hours on his nine hundred and eighty pound tiger shark, and I have heard of longer fights. No doubt I am due for a good licking, but that will be fun.

We raised a Marlin presently, and I ran back to the cockpit to coax this fellow to bite; and we had an exciting half-hour photographing and catching him—a good sized striped spearfish of two hundred and ninety pounds.

An American Angler in Australia

Not long after this event I sighted white splashes far to the southeast. I yelled to the boys, "Tuna splashes!"

We ran on, and in due time I saw dark patches on the smooth surface, and then schools of leaping bait fish, and then the gleaming flash of a leaping tuna in the air. He was big, too, easily one hundred and fifty pounds. Emil, who had seen this superb fish at Catalina, yelled his enthusiasm. There were scattered sharp splashes all over the sea. This meant tuna were feeding.

While Peter hooked up the engine and we bore down on these dark patches, I put on a tuna gig such as we use in the South Seas. Long before we reached the agitated waters I had a fine strike. Tuna always hook themselves. This one ran down and down, and had run four hundred yards of line off the reel before he slowed up.

I stopped him right *under* the boat, and then had some strenuous work pumping and winding him up. It required more than half an hour, that is, counting his narrowing circles under the boat. The sun was directly overhead, the sea perfectly calm, the water clear as crystal; and it was a striking picture to see that dazzling tuna as he came nearer and nearer to the boat.

I hoped that he would weigh a hundred pounds and cautioned Peter to make sure at the gaff. When hauled aboard this fish presented a most beautiful sight. He was a yellow-fin tuna, not to be confounded with the Australian and Western Pacific tunny; and the opal and blue

[37]

and gold colors, blending in a dazzling effect, as bright as sunlight on jewels, were so lovely that it seemed a shame to kill their possessor.

But this was a valuable catch, much more important than any size or species of swordfish. I was simply delighted.

In my correspondence for three years with Australian anglers and market fishermen I had been told of vast schools of large round blue fish that had been sighted offshore in July and August. These fish had been sighted, but not classified. I concluded they were tuna, and with this lucky catch I had verified my opinion.

Yellow-fin tuna furnish California with one of its big commercial assets—a fifty-million-dollar-a-year canned-tuna industry. There are floating canneries on the sea and canneries on shore. San Pedro, a thriving town, depends upon the tuna catch. For thirty years this business has been increasing. Large boats have been built, with refrigeration machinery and huge storage capacity, and these vessels ply far in pursuit of the schools of tuna. In 1927, when I found yellow-fin tuna at the Galapagos Islands, and showed motion pictures to verify it, the Japanese and American fleets were hot after these fresh schools. Five hundred tons of tuna, at a hundred dollars a ton, meant big profit.

Australian commercial interests have something to think about. It can be depended upon—these yellow-fin tuna are more and more in demand. Japanese ships now come clear to the Californian and Mexican coasts, and down off South America. It will be a close run to Australian waters.

The extent and abundance of this annual migration of yellow-fin tuna off the South Coast should be ascertained; and the result might well be a tremendous business for Australians, and what is more, a valuable and inexpensive food supply bound to take place of the more expensive meats. In the United States the consumption of fish as food has increased forty per cent in the last ten years.

CHAPTER V

~~~~~~

CROSSING THE RIVER ON THE FERRY AT BATE-
man Bay, from which the wonderful Toll
Gates can be seen out at sea, I conceived an idea
that this place had marvelous potentialities for
fishing. As a matter of fact, the place haunted me so that
I went back, motored all around the bay, walked out upon
the many wooded capes that projected far out toward the
sentinel Toll Gates, patrolled the curved sandy beaches,
and finally interviewed the market fishermen. The result
was that I broke camp at Bermagui and chose a lovely
site three miles out from Bateman Bay, where we
pitched camp anew. It turned out that the vision in my
mind's eye had been right. This camp was the most
beautiful and satisfactory of all the hundreds of camps
I have had in different countries. How it will turn out
from a fishing standpoint remains to be seen. But I would
like to gamble on my instinct.

I fished all the way up from Bermagui, and the distance must have been all of fifty miles. I trolled a good-
sized bonito for eight hours without a rise. The north-

east breeze had freshened the day, and at four o'clock the sea was ridged white and blue. It was rough enough to make me hold on to my chair with one hand and my rod in the other. I wanted to take the first swordfish in to Bateman Bay.

There was a long cape to the northwest, standing far out into the ocean. It appeared we would never reach it. But at last we did, and saw the grand opening of Bateman Bay guarded by those noble Toll Gates, great bare rocks, standing aloof and august, facing the sea, and shadowed with the western sunset lights.

It was with most unusual excitement that I sighted the familiar and thrilling purple flashes of a swordfish back of my bait. "There he is!" And he had the bait, to swerve and speed away.

"Well, it's about time. Nine hours!" called Peter, as he threw out the clutch. "Be sure you hook him."

I made sure of that, and for half an hour, in a rough sea, I had a hard fight with a game fish. He almost got away. We were proud to run into the little cove we had renamed Crescent Bay, where my camp had been pitched while I fished the day through.

There was an enthusiastic crowd waiting, but nothing to the large and vociferous one that greeted us when we trucked the swordfish up to town. Most, in fact almost all, of the inhabitants had never seen a swordfish. The reception the townspeople gave me was second only to what they gave the fish. So my start at Bateman Bay was auspicious.

Then, following that lucky opening, we had bad weather. Days of storm! No sooner would it clear up and give us hope of sunshine and warmth when it blew again. From all directions!

We ran out almost every day, certainly the days that it was possible to fish. We did not see a swordfish. I was not discouraged at this, because I have learned that patience and endurance are imperative for a deep-sea fisherman. Besides, we occasionally hooked a shark, and really I wanted a big shark more keenly than a swordfish.

After ten days the weather cleared and grew warm. That very first morning, drifting with a bait deep off Black Rock, I had a magnificent strike which I was sure came from a black Marlin. He took the bait easily, slowly made off, began to go faster and faster, and rise to the surface, until Peter and I yelled for the inevitable jump. It did not come. That fish got rid of the hook without leaping or showing his size; and I was a bitterly disappointed angler.

I did not, however, have long to bemoan my bad fortune. The camera-boat hooked up with a fish, and I couldn't miss that. There were always excitement and fun galore when my camera crew got hold of a fish. So I ran out to them. It would be quite beyond me to describe adequately what I witnessed. I shall record it in Bowen's terms:

"Gus Bagnard, my second camera man, was most eager to catch a swordfish. From his conversation I was sure that he thought it a simple matter, merely a case of tossing a bait overboard and pulling in the fish.

"He had been on the camera boat the day that I conceived the idea that if two teasers were good, more would be better. The idea may have been all right, but the execution was terrible. The extra teasers were tied with cord that had long since outlived its usefulness, and consequently kept breaking.

"A pleasant morning was had by all, in circling about, netting lost teasers. It was because of this that Gus hooked his swordfish.

"A teaser dropped off on the windward side and the boatman, forgetting all about the trailing lines, cut back so sharply that lines and teaser cords were twisting and twirling about, making a grand tangle. They missed the teaser on the first attempt at it, and again the boatman swung sharply, again not helping matters in the least. This occurred several times, and mind you the sea was quite rough. Suddenly I, who had been most busy keeping my bait from fouling, sighted a swordfish some distance in back. I yelled at Gus, whose bait was twisting around one of the teasers, to clear his line. Gus was making frantic effort to do so when the fish came up directly under his bait and swallowed it without ceremony.

"For some inexplicable reason Gus's line pulled free from the teaser and ran out with a mighty zip. In his excitement Gus forgot to keep enough tension on his reel and line was pouring all over the place. I jumped to his aid and between us we managed to pull out the loose overrun line, for the fish had by now conveniently stopped. Things were well in hand—that is except for the lost teaser which the boatman was still seeking. 'Stop the boat!' I yelled. Whether my voice did not carry or whether the boatman was going to get the teaser or bust, I never shall know, but at any rate they kept on, slowly of course, while the fish merely sulked on top of the water, shaking his head and paying little or no attention to Gus, who was pulling for all he was worth to take the slack out of his line.

"'Give me the harness!' Gus yelled. Thereupon Andy, my camera man, brought forth the harness and proceeded to help Gus put it on. Maybe it was the swaying of the boat, a gust of wind, putting on the harness, or all three things, but at any rate Gus's hat flew off his head and joined the teaser, which was floating by off the starboard.

"'I've got it!' yelled one of the boatmen, coming up with a dip net full of teaser. Just then the fish grew tired of this horseplay and made a wild rush out to sea. The boatman started after him, when Gus screamed, 'Hey, don't forget my hat!'

"I was laughing so hard by this time that I almost fell off the boat. The boatman, drawn between two evils, chose the lesser one and went after the hat. Gus was trying to keep a tight line on the fish while at the same time he was twisted around like an ostrich, in attempting to keep track of his hat.

"It might have been all right if the fish had continued to go one way and the boat the other, but just about the time they were nearing the hat, the fish looped back and came swimming towards the boat. The movement of the boat kept the line taut, but the fish in making the circle had evidently slacked enough of the line to free himself from the hook.

"'Here it is!' yelled the boatman as he dipped up the droopy hat. 'All right,' stated Gus, with relief. 'Now I'll show you how to catch this fish.' He reeled in hard and fast. Poor Gus, how he must have felt when he saw a baitless hook come dancing over the water. Anyway, he got his hat, the boatman got his teaser, and the rest of us got a laugh."

Following that event of the camera crew I trolled around and on out for an hour, when we discovered the other boat in trouble again. This time it proved to be Bowen who had gotten himself fast to a heavy fish. As soon as we had ascertained that, we trolled on, circling his boat at a goodly distance. As Brown did not make any apparent headway with this fish, we ran over again, to find him in sore straits.

That boat was not a comfortable one from which to fight a fish which had sounded deep. The chairs were wrong. There was a high railing on the stern which made it hazardous when a fish worked round astern. A sudden rush would snap the rod. If the fish sheered under the boat—well, then it was goodnight. Bowen was hunched on the side, his rod on the gunwale, the tip wagging, and the line stretched like a banjo string. Gus held him by the belt to keep him from being pulled overboard. In truth, he was in a grievous state, one I had suffered a thousand times. And it gave me a feeling of glee. I called through my megaphone:

"Ed, you've been on that fish two hours."

"Yaas!" bawled Bowen. "That's no news to me. What's it to you?"

"Your face is fearfully red and wet. Your shirt is coming off. And your efforts are appreciably ineffectual."

"Are you telling *me*?" yelled Ed, frantically. "Go 'way!"

"But you are doing a lot of things wrong," I protested.

"Oh, I am! Ha! Ha! For instance what?"

"If you want to hold a fish in that position or stop him, take hold of the line with both hands. If you can't do either, let him have line—let him run off so you can

[46]

straighten up—rest your arms—give him a chance to come to the surface, so you can have a different leverage."

"Aw!—look at that! He's taking line, millions of yards! —How'n hell will I ever reel him back?"

"Ed, listen," I called. "You don't *reel* a fish up. You pump him with the rod to get slack line—then you reel that. . . . But I'm afraid this fish is too much for you. He's licked you."

"He has—not!" panted Ed, wildly. "I've got him licked, only he won't come up. . . . Besides, it's no fish, I tell you. It's a whale or something."

"Ed, you betray every evidence of late hours, and cigarettes, the bottle, and in fact a misspent life. . . ."

"Go 'way!" shouted Bowen. "You'll make me so weak I'll lose him."

Bowen always claimed my advice would make him lose his fish. Wherefore I discreetly ran off, and trolled for two hours. Upon my return they had his fish tied up to the boat—a shark, of black hue and ferocious aspect, and of heavy frame. I did not know what kind it was.

"Hey there!" pealed out Ed, happily. "I got him! I got him! I licked the son-of-a-gun. Thanks for telling me what to do. Never would have licked him. Gee! but wasn't it a fight. I'm crippled. I'm dying!!! I think I'm dead. . . . What kind of a shark is it?"

"Blowed if I know," I replied, "But he's a handsome

[47]

brute, big as all outdoors, and a real catch. Congratulations."

This shark was indeed an important catch for us. It was a whaler and weighed over six hundred pounds.

On the following day, about sixteen miles offshore, out in a warm current that registered seventy-three degrees, I saw an enormous ghost-like shark that made my heart leap to my throat. He was twenty feet long and very deep, and he certainly was not afraid of the boat or its occupants. I let my bait out to him. It appeared to me that he not only ignored the offering, but was contemptuous of such a small bait. His eye was big, black, and gleaming with all the cold cruelty of nature. I knew that he saw me and would have taken *me* had I fallen out of that boat. For an hour after he faded away I was in a trance. I recovered after a time, but I will never cease to long to hook and whip and kill such a grand and terrible shark. Opinions on my boat differed. He was a tiger, or a huge whaler. But for me he was one of those monsters of the South Seas—the white death shark.

On the third clear morning, with a warm sun and a light northeast breeze, I felt sure that we would have luck. Peter said fish ought to be in. We found bait plentiful and hungry. While fishing around Black Rock I saw a Marlin jump. We got teasers and bait overboard in a hurry, and I trolled there for an hour, without raising him.

Meanwhile Bowen and his crew had run outside four or five miles. When I finally ran up to them they had a swordfish tied up to the boat. It had been caught by Mr. Stewart, a guest of Bowen's that day, and was his first one after many attempts. He appeared to be mute in his delight, but Bowen was gay and volatile enough.

"Say," he shouted, "you should have seen this Marlin commit suicide. Why, *nothing* could lose him! The reel overran a dozen times and never tangled. Get a load of that, will you? He ran under the boat. The leader caught in the propeller and the fish came up on the other side. All our backs were turned. He tried to get aboard. When we gaffed him the hook fell out. Can you beat that for luck?"

No, I could not, and after congratulating Mr. Stewart I trolled on, marveling at the queer angles of this game. Late in the afternoon we turned to go in. The golden lights were shining over the ranges, the purple Toll Gates loomed grandly against the background. The day appeared to be about over.

"There's a fin!" yelled Bill, suddenly. He was up on deck. "Far ahead and going fast."

"Chase it," I ordered. "Hook her up, Pete."

We ran down current like the wind, everybody searching the big swells and white seas. We ran nearly half a mile before Bill sighted the fin again. Still ahead! We ran on, lost it again. Then Emil saw it on our left and

[49]

we sped in that direction. We ran past the other boat. They yelled to us and pointed back to the right and we had to turn again. Peter saw him again and that encouraged us. He opened up the engine full ahead and we roared over the swells, leaving a white wake behind us.

"There he is!" shouted Peter, pointing. "Going like one thing!"

"Don't run him down, Peter," I said, as I caught my first glimpse of the big gleaming tail fin. "It's a black Marlin."

Peter slowed down. But we had to go at least at a ten-knot speed in order to come up with the fish. His tail went under, came up again, flashed opal and gold, vanished, to show once more.

Suddenly I saw that tail give a peculiar twitch—an action I had seen many times. I flashed my gaze back to my bait.

"He saw it! Look out!"

I venture to say that that fish traveled as fast as my sight. Because instantly there he was back of my bait. He snatched it and sheered off to the races. He ran four hundred yards on that strike, and when I hooked him he took off at least two hundred more. That was a long way off. The line was so tight I had to release the drag. We ran after him and it was quite awhile before I recovered a foot of line. He broke water twice, but did not leap.

Eventually we gained on him. In perhaps a quarter of

an hour I recovered most of the line. Then he sounded. From that period I fought him an hour and ten minutes to fetch him to the surface.

He proved to be a short, broad, beautifully built black Marlin, deep purple in color, and remarkable for the shortest spear I ever saw on one of these fish. It was less than a foot in length and a perfect weapon. This black Marlin weighed around four hundred pounds, and was I glad to take him in to Bateman Bay?

CHAPTER VI

~~~~~~

ONE OF MY STRONG REASONS FOR COMING TO Bateman Bay, if not the strongest, was the fact that this big shallow body of water was infested with sharks.

Salmon, bonito, yellowtail, taylor, mullet, which are the very best bait for any and all salt-water fish, inhabit this bay; and I am sure have a great deal to do with the presence of sharks.

After seeing a small specimen of wobbegong, or carpet shark, I was very keen to catch one. This fellow is about the most curious sea creature to be found. He resembles a long strip of Brussels carpet. He lies fairly flat on the bottom, almost like a flounder or halibut. He looks like seaweed and is a remarkable example of nature's protective coloration. But in his case it must be more a matter of hiding from the small fish he preys upon than to be difficult to see for his larger enemies. From the wobbegong's upper lip protrude a number of little colored bits of skin which could easily be taken for seaweed or something else good to eat. Anyway, this cunning shark lies low, watching, and when small fish come close to nibble at these deceitful lures the wobbegong snaps them up. This species of shark grows fairly large, and I'd give something unheard of to catch a big one. The most remarkable feature of the wobbegong is his teeth. They are like a nest of curved thorns. When the wobbegong gets his teeth in anything they cannot come free. They just bite out the piece they have hold of.

Sometimes when it was windy outside we ran in to fish around the islands or along the shoal west shore of the bay. Straight across from camp there was a high bluff covered with heavy growth of timber. From this a flat rocky reef ran out into the bay. Our man, Bill Lawler, the market fisherman I had engaged, took us often to this particular spot to fish for sharks. Some of the shark tales he told were incredible. But I learned to credit all of them.

Why a school of gray nurse sharks should hang around that shoal reef was a mystery to me. It cleared up, however, and seemed as natural as any other thing pertaining to the sea. We went there several times and chummed, (burley, they call this way of attracting sharks by cutting up bait or fish), without getting a single bite. Bill said the cool rainy weather accounted for the lack of sharks, and I could well believe him.

One warm still afternoon we hit it just right; and that afternoon must be recorded in my memory and in my fishing notes as one never to forget. Fishing for sharks is one thing: fishing for man-eating sharks, one of the most ferocious species, is entirely another.

I had seen the two gray nurse sharks in the Aquarium at the Sydney Zoo. I had watched them for hours. They really had beauty, if line and contour lending speed and savagery, can have such a thing. To my surprise the gray nurse had a longer, sharper nose than even the mako. I made a bet with myself that he could move fast in the water. I found out, too. I was surprised, also, to see that the gray nurse had no gray color in the water. He was a dark greenish tan.

We anchored the *Avalon* over the ridge, about five hundred yards out from shore, and began to chum. We had a couple of boxes full of fish that from its odor should have attracted sharks all the way from Sydney. Our other boat, the camera outfit, chose a spot half a mile below us, not a very good place, Bill said.

I put a bait over on my big tackle, and settled myself comfortably to wait. It was very pleasant, and grew more beautiful as the afternoon waned. Two hours passed, during which we chummed all the while, without having a strike. An oily slick drifted away from our boat for a mile. I had about decided there were no gray nurse sharks in the bay, when I had a bite. It was a gentle, slow pull, not at all what I expected from a notorious shark.

"It's a gray nurse," avowed Bill.

An American Angler in Australia

"Yeah?" I replied, doubtfully. "Okay! We'll hand it to him."

Whereupon I laid back with my heavy tackle for all I was worth. I hooked a fish, all right, and made ready for a run. But this one did not run. He came toward the boat. The men hauled up anchor and started the engine. We drifted while I most curiously applied myself to the task of whipping this shark, if it were one. He was heavy and strong, and quick as a flash. But he did not try to go places. He kept around and under the boat.

In due course I hauled him up, and what was my surprise when I saw a long symmetrical silver-gray shark shape. He looked about eight feet long and fairly thick. Presently I had a good look at his head and then his eyes. I have had fish see me from the water, but this fellow's gaze was different. Pure cold, murderous cruelty shone in that black eye. It made me shiver. I did not fool any longer with him.

Peter gaffed the gray nurse and held him while Bill slipped a rope over his tail. For his size, about three hundred pounds, he surely made a commotion in the water. After a bit Peter untied my leader from my line and let it hang. The shark hung head down, rolling and jerking.

"Pete, if these gray nurse sharks don't run away after being hooked, this tackle is too heavy," I said.

"Right-o. I was figuring that. The Cox nine and thirty thread line ought to do."

[55]

"Well," added Bill, grimly, "I can tell you they don't run away."

We went back to our anchorage and I went on fishing with the lighter rig while the men chummed. Suddenly Bill said he saw one in the water. I thought I, too, caught a gray shadow flash. But in a moment after that I had another of those queer slow gentle strikes.

"Gosh!" I exclaimed. "I'll bet this bird doesn't work so slow when he's after a man."

"Quick as lightning!" replied Bill.

The shark swam under the boat. I hooked him, and he acted precisely as had the first. But with the lighter tackle I could handle him better. He turned out to be heavy and strong, making it necessary for me to put on my harness. Then we had it out, hard and fast. Nevertheless I was able to do little with him. Had he chosen to run off we would have had to up anchor and go after him. But he chose to circle the boat and swim under it, giving me plenty of trouble. When I discovered the gray nurse wouldn't run I put on some drag and pitched into him. Several times I had a glimpse of something long and gray, like a ghost of a fish. In half an hour I had him coming. I did not see him clearly, however, until Peter had heaved on the leader. Then! what a thrill and a start! This one appeared a monster, eleven feet long, thick as a barrel, huge fins all over him, veritably a terrible en-gine of destruction. He would have weighed eight hundred pounds. Peter held the leader while Bill gaffed him. Then there was hell. The shark threw the gaff and bit through the leader in what appeared a single action.

"Oh, Peter!" I protested, in grievous disappointment. "He wasn't ready. Why didn't you let him go?"

Peter looked mad. Bill said not to mind, that there were more. This reassured me, and I asked for another leader. They were all twenty feet or more long, too long, but we had to use them.

"Look down there!" called Bill as I threw out my bait.

I did not look, because my bait had hardly sunk to the bottom, which was only three fathoms, when I had another of those slow electrifying tugs. When I hooked this gray nurse he nearly jerked the rod away from me and the rod-socket. By this time I was getting angry. I went after this one hammer and tongs. His action induced me to think he was trying to get to the boat and kill me. He never swam a dozen yards from where I sat. I put the wood on him, as we call hauling hard with the rod, and eventually whipped him and brought him up to the gaff. He nearly drowned me. And the boys were ringing wet and mad as wet hens. When Peter tied this one alongside the other they began to fight.

We rigged up another leader and I went at it again. This time Bill saw one before I threw my bait in.

"Look down," he directed, and pointed.

By peering over into the green water I saw long wavering shapes. Sharks! Gray nurse sharks, some of them nearly twelve feet long, swimming around over the chum we had distributed.

"My word! What a sight!" I ejaculated.

"Be careful the next one doesn't jerk you overboard," warned Bill.

"What'd they do?"

"Tear you to pieces!"

I well believed that, and I proceeded to fasten the snap below the reel so the rod could not be pulled away from the chair. In less than ten seconds after my bait disappeared I had a strike, and in another second I was fast again. It required about a quarter of an hour to lick the next one, around three hundred pounds in weight. We got him, tied him alongside his comrade; and his arrival started another fight.

The next two severed my leader, one at the gaff and the other was cut clean about the middle of the fight. That required other new leaders. This last was put on by Bill and my bait thrown overboard, when we heard a hard thumping behind us. Peter, the scalawag, had dropped a hook down on a heavy cord, and he was fast to a shark. He got the end of the leader up. The shark was a whopper and he roared around on the surface and banged against the boat.

"Help! Help!" yelled Peter.

Bill ran to his assistance just as I had another strike.

[58]

In a twinkling I was hooked to my heaviest gray nurse. He gave me a very hard battle. I needed my heavy outfit on him. But I was getting him well under control when Peter's shark swam under the boat and fouled my leader with his. In the mêlée that ensued Peter's shark broke away. I worked on mine awhile longer before I trusted him to Pete and Bill, whose blood was up and who had a lust to kill these man-eaters. No doubt mine was up, too, because I would have caught those devils until I was used up. This gray nurse was my largest to land. He weighed around five hundred pounds. When they tied him, head down, tail up, next to the other three, there was another convulsion. The boat cantled over and I had to hold on. Four gray nurse sharks in a row! And all possessed of devils! They did not appear to be sick or weak. They just fought.

"Peter, for Pete's sake let up on that hand-line stuff," I begged.

"Like hob I will," repeated my boatman.

"But you'll only foul my line."

"No matter. We'll ketch 'em."

And he had hold of another in less than ten seconds, even while Bill was baiting my hook. This time I watched. And I grasped that Peter would not give the sharks an inch of line. He sweat and swore and held on like grim death. The hook pulled out. Then I stood up to peer over the gunwale. Sharks thick as fence pickets!

[59]

But I could not see clearly. A few were small and many were about ten feet long, and several were very large. I wanted one of the biggest. My next was a smaller one, however, and I soon dragged him up. Peter had one on, too, and could not help us. Bill held the leader and the shark while I gaffed it. What a strange all-satisfying sensation, as the steel went in! But of course I was wholly primitive at the moment. The shark gave a wag and the gaff handle hit me on the head. I went down, not for the count, but to bounce up furious.

"Put a rope over his tail," yelled Bill.

"Don't do that," ordered Peter, aghast.

"Mind your own business," I replied. "Looks like you had your hands full."

Grasping up a tail rope, I widened the noose to bend over the gunwale and try to lasso that sweeping tail. I got the noose over, but before I could draw it tight he flipped it off. He bit at my hands and swept them aside as if they were paper. I was drenched to the skin. Then he hit me a resounding smack on the cheek and temple. Hurt? I was never so hurt in my life. Nor mad! I bent lower, grim and desperate.

"Look out!" yelled Bill. And before I could move he let go gaff and leader, and dragged me up. I had a glimpse of a gray flash, a cruel pointed nose. One of the devils had made a pass at me.

"My God! . . . Bill, did that shark . . . ?" I gasped.

"He did. Grab the rod and pull your shark back. . . . Afraid I've lost the gaff."

While I was pumping and winding my shark back Peter broke the heavy cord on the one he had hooked. That made him madder than ever. Bill ran forward to recover the gaff, which came out of the shark and floated up.

"I'll get one or bust," sang out Peter.

"This is a swell way to get rid of leaders," I replied. "But go to it. This will never happen again."

In less than a minute I was fast to another, and Pete's yell assured me he was, too.

Then things happened so quickly, and I was so confused with blood lust to kill sharks, and the excitement of the sport, that for a space I could not tell what was going on. There was tremendous exertion and much hoarse shouting, and especially a terrific splashing maelstrom when both my shark and the one Peter had hooked got tangled up with the four wicked ones we had tied to the boat.

That was a mess. It must be understood that the four live sharks were tied on the opposite side of the boat from which I was hanging on to the one I had hooked. My rod was bent double, mostly under the water. I had hold of my line with both gloved hands.

The men saved my shark, a good ten-footer, and lost Peter's, which he said was a whale. This time Peter cut

[61]

his hand on the leader, and therefore let up on his hand-line stuff. He had lost four. This helped matters somewhat, for the next and sixth one I hooked was not so hard to land. When he had been tied up on my side of the boat, the men tried to call me off. I indeed was spent and panting.

"Not on your life!" I yelled. "Not while they'll bite and I can lick 'em."

"They're thinning out," said Bill, gazing deep into the water. "But there's a big one, if you can get hold of him. . . ."

Marvelous to relate, I did, and he felt as if he was the granddad of that school of gray nurse sharks. He kept away from the boat for a while. He even came up, so that I could see all his wonderful silver-gray shape, his many fins, his gleaming eye and terrible shining teeth. This one was close to twelve feet long. He circled the stern, weaved to and fro, went under us time and again; in fact, he tried everything but to swim away. That was the strange thing. I could not understand it, unless he wanted to stay there to kill the thing which had him.

The sun was setting gold and blazing behind us on the wooded bluff. There were glorious lights and shadows on the Toll Gates. The water had a sheen of red, beautiful, though very significant of that afternoon's fight with man-eaters.

An American Angler in Australia

I was sure of this big one. Which conceit was foolish. I worked hard on him. I stopped him, or thought I had, time and again. All of a sudden, when he was almost under me, he made a quick lunge. I heard snaps. I felt released from a mighty pull. My tip, line, and harness strap all broke at once, and I fell back in the cockpit.

Next morning we hung my six gray nurse sharks on our tripod on the beach. I never felt such satisfaction and justification as that spectacle afforded me.

They were sleek, shiny gray, lean and wolfish, yet somehow had a fascinating beauty. The largest two weighed nearly five hundred pounds each.

Their noses and small eyes and curved teeth fascinated me most. There were six rows of these long curved teeth. Under the first row was the second, ready to bend a new tooth up when one was lost. It horrified me to think how often on Australian beaches this engine of destruction had buried such teeth in human flesh. Never again for one of these six, I thought, grimly! I'd rather catch and kill such bad sharks than land the gamest sporting fish that swims.

Lastly the many broad fins on these sharks nonplused me. There was a reason for them, but I could not figure it out at such short notice.

I regarded this catch as one of the greatest, and certainly the most worthy, that I ever made. And it was not until afterwards that I realized the hazard of the game, and that I had really not appreciated being in a den of blood-thirsty man-eaters. But instead of making me cautious I grew only the bolder, fierce to hook and fight the largest one I could find.

CHAPTER VII

ANY BOOK ON THE OUTDOORS, AT LEAST ANY ONE OF mine, should have as much as possible to say about trees, birds, and shells.

Our camp here is situated on a crescent-shaped bay, an offshoot of Bateman Bay, and it is singularly satisfying. All day and all night the surf is omnipresent, sometimes softly lapping the sand, at others crawling in with its white ripples, to break and seethe up the beach, rolling pebbles and shells with a tinkling music, and now and again rolling in with grand boom and roar, to crash on the strand and drag the gravel back with a mournful scream. A sad emotion-provoking sound on any shore!

Every tide leaves lines and patches and mounds of shells. Gathering shells is one of the great privileges of a fisherman, and I have accumulated over five hundred here, of many varieties. Shells have a singular appealing beauty. The search for new and different ones, for a perfect one of a certain kind, or a treasure just rolled up out of the unknown, grows in its fascination and adds many full moments to life, and pictures that will never fade from memory.

Birds here at Crescent Bay are rather few and far between. Even the sea birds are scarce. Gulls, terns, herons and cormorants frequent the shores, mostly early in the mornings. In the dark of dawn a trio of rascally kookaburras visit camp and set up a most raucous laughing, reverberating din in the giant trees, and then, having notified me that the break of day is at hand, they depart. They are not friendly here as were those at Bermagui. There are always ravens to be heard at odd moments of the day. These at Bateman Bay have the most dismal, grievous note I ever heard birds utter. They would be perfectly felicitous in Dante's Inferno. It is a hoarse, low, almost wild caw, penetrating, disturbing. You find yourself questioning your right to be happy—that calamity is abroad.

The magpies have a wonderful liquid, melodious note, somewhat similar to the beautiful one of the tui in New Zealand. The thrush sings rarely along this shore, and his call makes you stop to listen. There are other songsters that add to the joy of this camp site, but as I cannot identify them by their music alone they must go nameless.

Traveling to and fro along this south coast, I have made acquaintance with a number of trees, not many varieties, but countless ones of striking beauty. And it was my good fortune at this camp to pitch my tents under some of the grandest trees that ever ministered to me in my many needs of the changing hours of day and night.

They stand upon a sloping bench up from the beach some distance, and they dominate the scene. They are called spotted red gum trees. I could have thought of a better name than that, but it does not detract from their stately loveliness. There are about a dozen in number, four of which are giants of the bushland, ten feet thick at the base and towering two hundred feet aloft. They spread magnificently, huge branches sweeping out gnarled and crooked, but always noble with some quality of power and life and age. The lacy foliage gives the effect of a green canopy, with the sun's rays streaking down golden-green, as if through cathedral windows. But the color of these spotted monarchs intrigues me most. The dark spots and patches of bark stand out from a pale olive background that varies its hue according to the weather. In the rain the trunks take on a steely gray with black designs standing out in relief. At sunset, if there is gold and red in the west, these eucalyptus trees are indescribably beautiful. And on moonlight nights they are incredibly lovely. I have stared aloft for long, reveling in what it is they have so prodigally. I have watched the Southern Cross through a rift in the leaves. I have watched and loved them in the still noonday hour,

[67]

when not a leaf stirred, and have listened to them and trembled at their mighty threshing roar in the gale.

Trees must mean a great deal to man. He came down out of them, descending from his arboreal life, to walk erect on his feet, in that dim dawn of his evolution. And ever since, during that five hundred thousand years, he has been dependent upon them. And beyond material things, if man ever develops that far, he will need them to keep alive the spiritual, the beautiful, the something that nature stands for, the meaning which forever must be inscrutable.

Australians are blessed with their boundless bush. No doubt the bigness and warmth which are characteristic of the native Australian have come in some degree from the splendid trees under which he has lived.

It may seem rather a far cry from the beauty and ministry of trees to the ghastly menace of a man-eating shark, and a grueling fight with one, but that is where we must go.

South of Bateman Bay, and ten miles off Cape Burly, we ran into a trio of trawlers working a wide area of waters that must have netted them tons of fish. Many as have been the trawlers I have seen, I never before fished among them. This was a curious and unique experience, valuable to any fisherman.

These trawlers criss-crossed this twenty-mile square of ocean, and about every two hours they halted to haul up their nets. These had wooden doors, and an opening thirty or forty feet wide, which traveled along the bottom, scooping up all kinds of fish. We saw only the rubbish they threw overboard, consisting of small rays, fiddlers, sharks, porcupine fish, and a red-colored big-eyed fish that appeared to have burst upon the surface. We also saw barracuda, leatherjacks, and other fish.

They floated in confusion along the surface, in the track of the trawler, most of them alive, swimming upside down. Gulls, shearwater ducks (mutton birds), and the great wide-winged albatross reaped a harvest that the sharks had not time to get. The sharks, however, were busy enough. I saw dozens of whalers, a few hammerheads, several large pale sharks that kept deep down, and a number of Marlin in the wake of these ships.

It was exceedingly interesting to watch them, aside from the possibility of raising a swordfish. The screaming of the sea fowl, the colored fish lying scattered all over the wakes, the big dark fins and tails of sharks milling about, an occasional swirl and splash on the water, and lastly the passing to and fro of the trawlers afforded a moving and thrilling spectacle for an angler.

I took that all in as I trolled to and fro, following the ships. Swordfish fins were occasionally sighted, and we raised a number. They had fed, however, and would not take a bait, and their interest appeared to be solely in the teasers.

An American Angler in Australia

Two days of this working with the trawlers did not earn us a single Marlin. We caught several, though only after we had run far out of the zone of the trawlers. I tried a third day, however, finding it hard to resist those big sickle tails that we caught sight of rarely. I was, of course, on the lookout for a big black Marlin.

Still I kept a weather eye open for a big shark, and was not particular what breed he was. Among the trawlers it was not unusual to see a dozen whaler sharks all in a bunch, sticking their ugly dark noses out, gulping down fish into their wide mouths.

That third day, coming upon two big ones close together, I said to Emil, "Let's have a go at these." And we were soon fast to a heavy fish. A whaler will usually take a long fast run. Mine did this, while Emil's, evidently a huge fish, merely went down. Our boatman, Peter, was at a loss what to do. In the mêlée, however, Emil's shark got off, and I was left to battle a stubborn, heavy brute.

We caught up with him, and then he was off again. After this second run, however, he sounded deep and invited me to see what I could do about it. After an hour or so of getting him up and having him go down again I began to suspect that I had hold of a big fellow. Therefore I called upon patience and reserve strength to make a sure thing of catching him.

The fight was interesting because it was exactly what

An American Angler in Australia

Mr. Bullen, the Sydney shark expert, said was the way the great tiger worked. I was acquiring practice and experience, at considerable loss of sweat, labor, and enthusiasm. This son-of-a-gun stayed in one place, it appeared. I had to pump and wind, pump and wind, monotonously and continuously. I would get him up to the double line and then down he would go again. I had that work to do over and over. His evident size, however, kept me nailed to my post; and after over two hours of hard work I had him coming.

My first sight of this whaler was a flash of gold, and as he came closer up he changed color from that to dark green, and finally black. He was a sullen-eyed surly brute that made striking the gaff into him a keen, savage sort of pleasure. When Peter sent the steel home I yelled, "Mr. Whaler, *you'll* never kill another human being!"

That idea had seemed to obsess me all along, and it grew stronger. This whaler was big and heavy and mean. On the gaff he raised hell, wet us thoroughly, and made everybody mad. He was too big to haul up on the stern, so we had to tow him fifteen miles to camp—a long, slow trip.

I gambled with the boys on his weight, which I wagered was nine hundred pounds, but, as usual, I lost, for he weighed only eight hundred and ninety. He was twelve feet long; and those two facts constitute a mighty big fish.

An American Angler in Australia

A Mr. Wallace and companion fisherman, staying at Bateman Bay, came in one day with a six-hundred-and-ninety-pound shark, which they had fought for forty minutes, and then shot. They could not identify it, and asked me to do so, which I was glad to be able to do. Sharks can always be identified by their teeth, provided you know shark teeth.

Fortunately, in this case it was easy, as the large triangular upper teeth, serrated, and the smaller less-triangular lower teeth, belonged to that rare species of the Seven Seas—the white pointer or less commonly known as the white death.

This fellow grows to forty feet and more in length, and teeth have been found in the ooze from the bottom of the sea so large that they must have belonged to sharks eighty feet long—a fearful and marvelous monster to conjure up in imagination.

I had seen at least two of these rare and great sharks, one at Rangaroa, in the Paumotos, and the other off Montague Island. Naturally I was hoping to catch one.

So far as I can ascertain, only three of this species has been caught in Australia, one eighteen feet long, shot and harpooned at Bermagui; another larger, which was vouched for by Dr. Stead, the scientist. My boatman, Peter Williams, harpooned one at the whaling-station near Russell, New Zealand. It was twenty-three feet long and would have weighed far over a ton. I saw the jaws of this one, and they were indeed formidable. A good-sized man could sit down inside of them.

My hopes of striking a white-death shark on the South Coast had almost waned when, three days before we shifted camp at Bateman Bay I sighted what I thought was one at Black Rock. He had the same shape and the same dorsal fin with which I had familiarized myself. Only he appeared darker in color.

Peter was not keen about closer acquaintance, but that certainly did not hold for me. I cautioned him to keep wide as we dragged a freshly cut salmon across in front of the shark. If the fish saw it he gave no sign. Again we ran in front of the brute and closer this time. In fact we went pretty close. I saw his peculiarly blunt nose, coming to a point, and the protruding upper lip which allowed the big white arrowhead-shaped teeth to show. That was a sight to chill the blood. He was lazily riding the waves, his bold, staring black eyes on the boat. Surely he saw us. But he ignored the bait.

"Throw something at the blighter," yelled Peter.

"Nope. Go closer next time," I replied.

On this third attempt, before we got even with the shark, he made a swift and savage run. There was a splash, a crack, and he sheered away swift as a Marlin. The instant I recovered from this surprising procedure I jammed on the drag and struck. If that shark did anything, he struck back at me. Then, when I had him

[73]

hooked, he performed the old amazing, thrilling trick of the mako—he came for us. I had to wind fast to reel in the line.

There he was! Only the length of my leader! And that was thirty feet.

"What'll we do now?" I shouted, aghast.

"Hang on to the double line," replied Peter, and dived into the cabin for the gaff.

The swivel of the leader was against my rod tip. I had no trouble in holding the shark. He turned at right angles with us and was swimming along with the boat, a few feet under. Presently he came up so that his pale dorsal fin stood up out of the water. He was not white by any means, but he was light colored, and stream-lined in shape, and sinister of aspect. He looked large, too, fully as large as my biggest whaler.

"Pete, what are you going to do?" I called, as he came out with gaff and rope.

"Let's have a go at him."

"It's too soon. If you failed to get the gaff in good he'd drown us and get away."

On the other hand, if we hurt him and he ran off, it was almost a certainty that he would take long to drag in again. I debated the question. If it had not been a white shark I would not have hesitated. But during that moment of vacillation the shark made up his mind and he ran off two hundred yards as fast as any Marlin ever went. Then he stopped, but did not sound. He just fought the leader; and as I put all my weight and strength into the task we had it nip and tuck. I could always fight a fish far away from me better than one near at hand. For my pains, however, I got very little line in.

"Shall I run up on him?" asked Peter.

"No. I'll pull him back or break him off," I replied as, baffled and resentful, I worked with renewed vigor. I did not keep track of the time, but it was far from being short. I had enough of this white shark to guess at what a twenty-footer would be like. And in due course, when I pulled the leader up within reach, I was wet and panting, and mad at my ineffectual attempt.

He went under the boat, so we had to keep moving. Peter hauled on the leader in a way to alarm me. And he was swearing, always with Peter a sign of impatience and effort. Emil stood with the big gaff, ready to hand it to the boatman, while I loosened my harness hooks, and the drag on the reel.

"Drop the leader overboard," I cautioned, as always.

I saw the shark come out from under the boat. He had rolled over on the leader. The bright steel flashed. Crash! Then all was lost in a maelstrom of flying white spray and green water.

"Let him run on the rope," I shouted.

"I can hold him. . . . Emil, get a tail rope," replied Peter.

An American Angler in Australia

It required some time to put a noose over that thresh-ing tail, during which I stood there, ready to carry on my part should the shark break away. Once roped, however, he gave up with little more ado.

We tried to haul him up on the stern, but he was too heavy. We, therefore, towed him the three miles in to camp. Night had fallen when we arrived, so that we could neither weigh nor photograph him. The boys pulled him up on the bank, however, and left him there. After supper I went to look at him, finding him dead and growing dark in color. He appeared to be a soft-fleshed shark that would shrink much overnight.

Next morning we stayed in camp a few hours to photo-graph this specimen. He was not so large, though nearly so, as my big whaler. And allowing for the percentage of shrinkage he weighed eight hundred and forty pounds. And he was nine feet six inches long. He had turned a grayish black in color. His pectorals were large. His round lower end, and the flange where it joined the tail, resembled that of both a mako and a broadbill sword-fish, but more like the latter fish. Close study of this shark identified it as immature. He really was a youngster of that species. But for me he was a notable catch, a differ-ent and splendid shark, and I was proud of having gotten him and adding that terrible white-fanged jaw to my collection. I made a reluctant and secret observation, too, and it was that I was going to be scared of a giant shark of his class.

CHAPTER VIII

FASCINATING PLACES TO FISH HAVE BEEN A specialty of mine; and I have record of many where no other fisherman ever wet a line. This always seemed to be a fetish of mine. New and lonely waters! My preference has been the rocky points of islands where two currents meet.

Fishing off Sydney Heads, Australia, is as far removed from this as could well be imagined.

Great scarred yellow cliffs, like the colored walls of an Arizona canyon, guard the entrance to Sydney Harbor, which, if not really the largest harbor in the world, is certainly the most wonderful. These bold walls, standing high and sheer, perhaps a mile apart, look down upon the most colorful and variable shipping of the Seven Seas. I passed through this portal on the S.S. *Mariposa*, gazing up at the lofty walls, at the towering lighthouses and the slender wireless stands black against the sky, never dreaming that the day would come when I saw them above me while fighting one of the greatest giant fish I ever caught.

At the end of three months fishing on the South Coast

of Australia, during which my party and I caught sixty-seven big fish, mostly swordfish, weighing twenty-one thousand pounds, we found ourselves at Watson's Bay, just around the corner of the South Head, within sight of all Sydney, and in fact located in the city suburbs, for the purpose of pursuing further our extraordinary good luck. I hoped, of course, to catch the first swordfish off Sydney Heads, and incidentally beat the shark record.

I was introduced to this Sydney fishing by Mr. Bullen, who held the record, and who had pioneered the rod-and-reel sport practically alone, and had been put upon his own resources and invention to master the hazardous and hard game of fishing for the man-eating tiger shark.

In angling, my admiration and respect go to the man who spends much time and money and endurance in the pursuit of one particular fish. Experiment and persistence are necessary to the making of a great angler. If Mr. Bullen has not arrived, he surely is far on the way. For three years he fished for tiger sharks from boats which in some cases were smaller than the fish he fought. His mistakes in method and his development of tackle were but steps up the stairway to success. I want to record here, in view of the small craft he fished out of and the huge size and malignant nature of tiger sharks, that, after a desperate battle to bring one of these man-eaters up to the surface, he was justified in shooting it.

This shooting of sharks, by the way, was the method

practiced in Australia, as harpooning them was and still is prevalent in New Zealand. In America we have sixty years' development back of big-game fishing; and all the sporting clubs disqualify a harpooned or shot fish. The justification of this rule is that opportunity presents very many times to kill a big fish or shark before it has actually waked up. This is not fair to the angler who fights one for a long time.

In Australia, however, the situation is vastly different. There are thousands of terrible sharks. In the book I am writing, *Tales of Man-eating Sharks,* I have data for three hundred tragedies and disasters. I expect this book will be a revelation to those distinguished scientists of the United States who do not believe a shark will attack a human being. Certainly it would be better to fish for sharks and shoot them on sight than not fish at all. For, every shark killed may save one or more lives. While I have been in Australia there have been several tragedies, particularly horrible. A boy bathing at Manly Beach was taken and carried away for moments in plain sight. Somewhere in South Australia another boy was swimming near a dock. Suddenly a huge blue pointer shark seized him and leaped clear of the water with him, before making off. Such incidents should make a shark-killer out of any angler.

Before I reached Sydney I had caught a number of man-eaters, notably some whalers, an unknown white shark, and some of those sleek, treacherous devils, the gray nurse, believed by many to be Australia's most deadly shark. I had had enough experience to awaken in me all the primitive savagery to kill which lay hidden in me, and I fear it was a very great deal. The justification, however, inhibits any possible thought of mercy. Nevertheless, despite all the above, I think gaffing sharks is the most thrilling method, and the one that gives the man-eater, terrible as he is, a chance for his life. If you shoot a shark or throw a Norway whale harpoon through him, the battle is ended. On the other hand, if by toil and endurance, by pain and skill, you drag a great shark up to the boat, so that your boatman can reach the wire leader and pull him close to try and gaff him, the battle by no means is ended. You may have to repeat this performance time and again; and sometimes your fish gets away, after all. Because of that climax I contend that all anglers should graduate to the use of the gaff. Perhaps really the very keenest, fiercest thrill is to let your boatman haul in on the leader and *you* gaff the monster. Thoreau wrote that the most satisfying thing was to strangle and kill a wild beast with your naked hands!

It was only a short run by boat round the South Head to the line of cliff along which we trolled for bait. The water was deep and blue. Slow swells heaved against the rocks and burst into white spray and flowed back into the sea like waterfalls. A remarkable feature was the huge flat ledges or aprons that jutted out at the base of the walls, over which the swells poured in roaring torrent, to spend their force on the stone face and slide back in glistening maelstrom. Dr. Stead assures me this apron is an indication of very recent elevation of the coast. The Gap was pointed out to me where a ship struck years ago on a black stormy night, to go down with all of the hundreds on board, except one man who was lifted to a rock and, crawling up, clung there to be rescued. Suicide Leap was another interesting point where scores of people had gone to their doom, for reasons no one can ever fathom. The wooden ladders fastened precariously on the cliff, down to the ledges where fishing was good, these that had been the death of so many fishermen, held a singular gloomy fascination for me.

Trolling for bait was so good that I did not have so much time for sight-seeing. Bonito and kingfish bit voraciously and we soon had plenty of bait. We ran out to sea dragging teasers and bonito in the wake of the *Avalon*, and I settled down to that peculiar happiness of watching the sea for signs of fish. Hours just fade away unnoticeably at such pastime. In the afternoon we ran in to the reefs and drifted for sharks.

I derived a great deal of pleasure from watching the ships that passed through the harbor gate and those which came out to spread in all directions, according to their destinations, all over the world, and soon grow hull down on the horizon and vanish. Airplanes zoomed overhead. Small craft dotted the green waters outside and white sails skimmed the inner harbor. Through the wide gate I could see shores and slopes covered with red-roofed houses, and beyond them the skyscrapers of the city, and dominating all this scene the grand Sydney bridge, with its fretwork span high above the horizon.

It was a grand background for a fishing setting. At once I conceived an idea of photographing a leaping swordfish with Sydney Heads and the gateway to the harbor, and that marvelous bridge all lined against the sky behind that leaping fish. That day was futile, however, much to Mr. Bullen's disappointment. The next day was rough. A hard wind ripped out of the northeast; the sea was ridged blue and white; the boat tipped and rolled and dived until I was weary of hanging on to my seat and the rod. We trolled all over the ocean for hours, until afternoon, then came in to drift off the Heads. Still, somehow, despite all this misery there was that thing which holds a fisherman to his task. When I climbed up on the dock I had the blind staggers and the floor came up to meet me. The usual crowd was there to see me, but I could not sign any autographs that night.

The third morning dawned warm and still, with a calm ocean and blue sky. Starting early, we trolled for bait along the bluffs as far south as Point Bondi. I had engaged the services of Billy Love, market fisherman and shark-catcher of Watson's Bay, to go with us as guide to the shark reefs. We caught no end of bait, and soon were trolling off Bondi. We ran ten miles out, and then turned north and ran on until opposite Manly Beach, where we headed in again to run past that famous bathing-beach where so many bathers had been attacked by sharks, and on down to Love's shark-grounds directly opposite the harbor entrance between the Heads, and scarcely more than a mile outside the Heads.

We put down an anchor, or "killick," as our guide called it, in about two hundred feet of water. A gentle swell was moving the surface of the sea. The sun felt hot and good. Putting cut bait overboard, we had scarcely settled down to fishing when we had a strike from a small shark. It turned out to be a whaler of about three hundred pounds.

Love was jubilant over its capture.

"Shark meat best for sharks," he avowed, enthusiastically. "Now we'll catch a tiger sure!"

That sharks were cannibals was no news to me, but in this instance the fact was more interesting. Emil put a bonito bait over and Love attached a little red balloon to the line a fathom or two above the leader. This was Mr. Bullen's method, except that he tied the float about one hundred and fifty feet above the bait, and if a strong current was running he used lead.

For my bait Love tied on a well-cut piece of shark,

about two pounds in weight, and added what he called a fillet to hang from the point of the hook. I was an expert in baits and I remarked that this one looked almost good enough to eat.

Then he let my bait down twenty-five fathoms without float or sinker. This occurred at noon, after which we had lunch, and presently I settled down comfortably to fish and absorb my surroundings.

The sun was hot, the gentle motion of the boat lulling, the breeze scarcely perceptible, the sea beautiful and compelling, and there was no moment that I could not see craft of all kinds, from great liners to small fishing-boats. I sat in my fishing-chair, feet on the gunwale, the line in my hand, and the passage of time was unnoticeable. In fact, time seemed to stand still.

The hours passed, until about mid-afternoon, and conversation lagged. Emil went to sleep, so that I had to watch his float. Peter smoked innumerable cigarettes, and then he went to sleep. Love's hopes of a strike began perceptibly to fail. He kept repeating about every hour that the sharks must be having an off day. But I was quite happy and satisfied.

I watched three albatross hanging around a market boat some distance away. Finally this boat ran in, and the huge white-and-black birds floated over our way. I told Love to throw some pieces of bait in. He did so, one of which was a whole bonito with its sides sliced off. The albatross flew towards us, landed on their feet a dozen rods away, and then ran across the water to us. One was shy and distrustful. The others were tame. It happened, however, that the suspicious albatross got the whole bonito, which he proceeded to gulp down, and it stuck in his throat.

He drifted away, making a great to-do over the trouble his gluttony had brought him. He beat the water with his wings and ducked his head under to shake it violently.

Meanwhile the other two came close, to within thirty feet, and they emitted strange low, not unmusical, cries as they picked up the morsels of fish Love pitched them. They were huge birds, pure white except across the back and along the wide-spreading wings. Their black eyes had an Oriental look, a slanting back and upwards, which might have been caused by a little tuft of black feathers. To say I was in a seventh heaven was putting it mildly. I awoke Emil, who, being a temperamental artist and photographer, went into ecstasies with his camera. "I can't believe my eyes!" he kept exclaiming. And really the lovely sight was hard to believe, for Americans who knew albatross only through legend and poetry.

Finally the larger and wilder one that had choked over his fish evidently got it down or up and came swooping down on the others. They then engaged in a fight for the pieces our boatman threw them. They ate a whole bucketful of cut bonito before they had their fill, and one of them was so gorged that he could not rise from the surface. He drifted away, preening himself, while the others spread wide wings and flew out to sea.

Four o'clock found us still waiting for a bite. Emil had given up; Peter averred there were no sharks. Love kept making excuses for the day, and like a true fisherman kept saying, "We'll get one tomorrow." But I was not in a hurry. The afternoon was too wonderful to give up. A westering sun shone gold amid dark clouds over the Heads. The shipping had increased, if anything, and all that had been intriguing to me seemed magnified. Bowen, trolling in Bullen's boat, hove in sight out on the horizon.

My companions obviously gave up for that day. They were tired of the long wait. It amused me. I remarked to Peter: "Well, old top, do you remember the eighty-three days we fished without getting a bite?"

"I'll never forget that," said Pete.

"And on the eighty-fourth day I caught my giant Tahitian striped marlin?"

"Right, sir," admitted Peter.

Love appeared impressed by the fact, or else what he thought was fiction, but he said, nevertheless: "Nothing doing today. We might as well go in."

"Ump-umm," I replied, in cowboy parlance. "We'll hang a while longer."

I did not mention that I had one of my rare and singular feelings of something about to happen. My companions settled down resignedly to what seemed futile carrying-on.

Fifteen minutes later something took hold of my line with a slow irresistible pull. My heart leaped. I could not accept what my eyes beheld. My line slowly payed off the reel. I put my gloved hand over the moving spool in the old habit of being ready to prevent an overrun. Still I did not believe it. But there—the line slipped off slowly, steadily, potently. Strike! There was no doubt of that. And I, who had experienced ten thousand strikes, shook all over with the possibilities of this one. Suddenly, sensing the actuality, I called out, *"There he goes!"*

Peter dubiously looked at my reel—saw the line gliding off.

"Right-o, sir!"

Love's tanned image became radiant. Emil woke up and began to stutter.

"It's a fine strike," yelled Love, leaping up. "Starts like a tiger!"

He ran forward to heave up the anchor. Peter directed Emil to follow and help him. Then I heard the crack of the electric starter and the sound of the engine.

"Let him have it!" advised Peter, hopefully. "It was a long wait, sir. . . . Maybe . . . "

"Swell strike, Pete," I replied. "Never had one just like it. He has taken two hundred yards already. It feels under my fingers just as if you had your hand on my coat sleeve and were drawing me slowly toward you."

"Take care. He may put it in high. And that anchor line is long."

When Love and Emil shouted from forward, and then came running aft, the fish, whatever it was, had out between four and five hundred yards of line. I shoved forward the drag on the big Kovalovsky reel and struck with all my might. Then I reeled in swift and hard. Not until the fifth repetition of this violent action did I come up on the weight of that fish. So sudden and tremendous was the response that I was lifted clear out of my chair. Emil, hands at my belt, dragged me back.

"He's hooked. Some fish! Get my harness," I rang out.

In another moment, with my shoulders sharing that pull on me, I felt exultant, deeply thrilled, and as strong as Samson. I quite forgot to look at my watch, which seemed an indication of my feelings. My quarry kept on taking line even before I released the drag.

"Run up on him, Pete. Let's get close to him; I don't like being near these anchored boats."

There were two fishing-boats around, the nearer a little too close for comfort. Peter hooked up the engine and I bent to the task of recovering four hundred yards of line. I found the big Kovalovsky perfect for this necessary job. I was hot and sweating, however, when again I came up hard on the heavy weight, now less than several hundred feet away and rather close to the surface.

I watched the bend of my rod tip.

"What kind of fish?" I asked.

"It's sure no black Marlin," answered Peter, reluctantly.

"I couldn't tell from the rod," added Love. "But it's a heavy fish. I hope a tiger."

Emil sang out something hopeful. I said: "Well, boys, it's a shark of some kind," and went to work. With a medium drag I fought that shark for a while, watching the tip, and feeling the line, to get what we call "a line" on him. But it was true that I had never felt a fish just like this one. One instant he seemed as heavy as a rock, and the next light, moving, different. Again I lost the feel of him entirely, and knowing the habit of sharks to slip up on the line to bite it, I reeled like mad. So presently I was divided between the sense that he was little, after all, and the sense that he was huge. Naturally I gravitated to the conviction that I had hooked a new species of fish to me, and a tremendously heavy one. My plan of battle therefore was quickly decided by that. I shoved up the drag on the great Kovalovsky reel to five pounds, six, seven pounds. This much had heretofore been a drag I had never used. But this fish pulled each out just as easily as if there had been none. I could not hold him or get in any line without following him. So cautiously I pushed up the drag to nine pounds, an unprecedented power for me to use. It made no difference at all to the fish, wherefore I went back to five pounds. For a while I ran after him, wound in the line, then had the boat stopped and let him pull out the line again.

"I forgot to take the time. Did any of you?"

"About half an hour," replied Emil.

"Just forty minutes," said Peter, consulting his clock in the cabin. "And you're working too fast—too hard. Ease up."

I echoed that forty minutes and could hardly believe it. But time flies in the early stages of a fight with a big fish. I took Peter's advice and reduced my action. And at this stage of the game I reverted to the conduct and talk of my companions, and to the thrilling facts of the setting. Peter held the wheel and watched my line, grim and concerned. Love bounced around my chair, eager, talkative, excited. Emil sang songs and quoted poetry while he waited with his camera. Occasionally he snapped a picture of me.

The sea was aflame with sunset gold. A grand golden flare flooded through the gate between the Heads. Black against this wonderful sky the Sydney Bridge curved aloft over the city, majestic, marvelous in its beauty. To its left the sinking sun blazed upon the skyscraper buildings. The black cliffs, gold rimmed, stood up boldly far above me. But more marvelous than any of these, in fact exceedingly rare and lovely to me, were the ships putting to sea out of that illuminated gateway. There were six of these in plain sight.

"Getting out before Good Friday," said Peter. "That one on the right is the *Monowai*, and the other on the left is the *Maunganui*. They're going to come to either side of us, and pretty close."

"Well!" I exclaimed. "What do you think of that? I've been on the *Monowai* and have had half a dozen trips in the *Maunganui*."

These ships bore down on us, getting up speed. The officers on the bridge of the *Maunganui* watched us through their glasses, and both waved their caps. They must have recognized the *Avalon*, and therefore knew it was I who was fast to a great fish right outside the entrance of Sydney Harbor. The deck appeared crowded with curious passengers, who waved, and cheered. That ship steamed hissing and roaring by us, not a hundred yards away, and certainly closer to my fish than we were. The *Monowai* passed on the other side, almost even with her sister ship. Naturally, being human, I put on a show for these ships, by working hard and spectacularly on my fish.

Close behind these loomed a ship twice as large. She appeared huge in comparison. From her black bulk gleamed myriads of lights, and vast clouds of smoke belched from her stacks. Peter named her, the *Rangitati*, or some name like that, and said she was bound for England via the Panama Canal. Then the other ships came on and passed us, and soon were silhouetted dark against the purple sky.

All this while, which seemed very short and was perhaps half an hour, I worked on my fish, and I was assured that he knew it. Time had passed, for the lighthouse on the cliff suddenly sent out its revolving piercing rays. Night was not far away, yet I seemed to see everything almost as clearly as by day.

For quite a space I had been able to get the double line over the reel, but I could not hold it. However, I always tried to. I had two pairs of gloves and thumb stalls on each hand; and with these I could safely put a tremendous strain on the line without undue risk, which would have been the case had I trusted the rod.

By now the sport and thrill had been superseded by pangs of toil and a grim reality of battle. It had long ceased to be fun. I was getting whipped and I knew it. I had worked too swiftly. The fish was slowing and it was a question of who would give up first. Finally, without increasing the strain, I found I could stop and hold my fish on the double line. This was occasion for renewed zest. When I told my crew they yelled wildly. Peter had long since got out the big detachable gaff, with its long rope.

I held on to that double line with burning, painful

hands. And I pulled it in foot by foot, letting go to wind in the slack.

"The leader—I see it!" whispered Love.

"*Whoopee!*" yelled Emil.

"A little more, sir," added Peter, tensely, leaning over the gunwale, his gloved hands outstretched.

In another moment I had the big swivel of the leader in reach.

"Hang on—Pete!" I panted, as I stood up to release the drag and unhook my harness. "Drop the leader—overboard. . . . Emil, stand by. . . . Love, gaff this fish when I—tell you!"

"He's coming, sir," rasped out Peter, hauling in, his body taut. "There! . . . *My Gawd!*"

Emil screeched at the top of his lungs. The water opened to show the back of an enormous shark. Pearl gray in color, with dark tiger stripes, a huge rounded head and wide flat back, this fish looked incredibly beautiful. I had expected a hideous beast.

"*Now!*" I yelled.

Love lunged with the gaff. I stepped back, suddenly deluged with flying water and blindly aware of a roar and a banging on the boat. I could not see anything for moments. The men were shouting hoarsely in unison. I distinguished Peter's voice. "*Rope—tail!*"

"*Let him run!*" I shouted.

Between the up-splashing sheets of water I saw the

three men holding that shark. It was a spectacle. Peter stood up, but bent, with his brawny shoulders sagging. Love and Emil were trying to rope that flying tail. For I had no idea how long, but probably a brief time, this strenuous action prevailed before my eyes. It beat any battle I recalled with a fish at the gaff. The huge tiger rolled over, all white underneath, and he opened a mouth that would have taken a barrel. I saw the rows of white fangs and heard such a snap of jaws that had never before struck my ears. I shuddered at their significance. No wonder men shot and harpooned such vicious brutes!

"It's over—his tail," cried Love, hoarsely, and straightened up with the rope. Emil lent a hand. And then the three men held that ferocious tiger shark until he ceased his struggles. They put another rope over his tail and made fast to the ring-bolt.

When Peter turned to me his broad breast heaved—his breath whistled—the corded muscles stood out on his arms—he could not speak.

"Pete!—Good work. I guess that's about the hardest tussle we've ever had at the gaff."

We towed our prize into the harbor and around to the dock at Watson's Bay, where a large crowd awaited us. They cheered us lustily. They dragged the vast bulk of my shark up on the sand. It required twenty-odd men to move him. He looked marble color in the twilight. But the tiger stripes showed up distinctly. He knocked men right and left with his lashing tail, and he snapped with those terrible jaws. The crowd, however, gave that business end of him a wide berth. I had one good long look at this tiger shark while the men were erecting the tripod; and I accorded him more appalling beauty and horrible significance than all the great fish I had ever caught.

"Well, Mr. Man-eater, you will never kill any boy or girl!" I flung at him.

That was the deep and powerful emotion I felt—the justification of my act—the worthiness of it, and the pride in what it took. There, I am sure, will be the explanation of my passion and primal exultance. Dr. Stead, scientist and official of the Sydney Museum, and Mr. Bullen of the Rod Fishers' Society, weighed and measured my record tiger shark. Length, thirteen feet ten inches. Weight, one thousand and thirty-six pounds!

CHAPTER IX

⌇⌇

A S LUCK WOULD HAVE IT, MY MANAGER, ED Bowen, had the honor of catching the first striped Marlin swordfish ever brought in to Sydney. The feat pleased me almost as much as if I had done it myself.

We had seen several swordfish tails cutting the swells off Sydney Heads, from three to ten miles out, and we were satisfied that we could catch some Marlin if only we had some good weather. But out of three weeks at Watson's Bay we had only a few days when we could fish. And it so happened that the day I caught a five-hundred-and-forty-pound whaler shark and an eight-hundred-and-five-pound tiger was the one on which Bowen snagged the coveted prize of the first Marlin for Sydney.

He deserved credit for it, too. The sea was rough out wide, as the Australians call offshore, and he followed my pet method of running the wheels off the boat. Fishing out of Bullen's boat, with the genial Erroll as companion, Bowen ran along the cliffs, catching bait as far down as Bondi, then struck out to sea. Twelve miles or so out they hit into that warm blue south-bound current I have mentioned so often, and trolled to and fro, up and down, from ten until three without a rise.

About three, however, Bowen saw a blue streak shooting in toward bait and teasers. He yelled lustily. Bullen then saw the fish and swiftly reeled in his bait. It was an even break for the anglers, both baits abreast, with fame for the lucky one. Bullen's action would be incredible under ordinary circumstances, but considering that he had started the big-game fishing at Sydney, and had been three years trying and learning under many handicaps, this sporting deed, this generous sacrifice, was one of singular and extraordinary self-effacement and sportsmanship. I have done this trick a few times in my life, mostly for my brother R. C., but I doubt that I could have done it in this peculiar case.

The Marlin was ravenous, and gobbling Bowen's bait he was off to the races. Bowen said he had never been so keen, so tense to hook a fish, and that he had the thrill of his life when he came up on the weight of the Marlin. This Marlin was one of the wild ones and ran and jumped all over the ocean. In due course Ed whipped this fish and Bullen gaffed it. With the beautiful purple-striped specimen on board they headed for Sydney Harbor, and ran in to Watson's Bay just before sunset. The fish was weighed in before a record crowd, and registered one hundred and seventy-two pounds. The size, however, had nothing to do with the importance of the event. Telephones began to buzz and in an hour all the reporters in Sydney were on the job. The feat was heralded as it deserved. Before eight o'clock every vestige of that Marlin, except the backbone, was gone, for souvenirs and morsels of meat to cook.

Even before the capture of this game species of sporting fish, I had already envisioned Watson's Bay, Sydney, as one of the great fishing-resorts of the world. I can see a fine hotel and cottages go up in that delightful bay, and many high-powered fast launches with capable boatmen to take care of the anglers from overseas.

Australians, with few exceptions, will go slowly for this new sport. They have not been born to it. Nothing has been known of the swordfish, and the great sharks were considered as vermin, hardly worth the use of a hand line. But the overseas anglers will change all this. Their experience, their reputation, their fishing-gear, and their incredible passion for the game will intrigue the hundreds of rich sportsmen in Australia, and excite in them a spirit of rivalry. "Here," they will say, "what's all this about? All this expense and persistence. What are we missing?"

The big sharks will interest the overseas fishermen. Every last one of them will want to capture a huge tiger shark. Personally, I don't see anything lacking in this tiger to make him a prize. He is a strong, heavy, mean fighter. He is full of surprises. He is huge and frightful, beautiful and savage in the water, and terrible out of it. If, in any particular case, there is something lacking in this tiger shark, it is more than made up for by the nature of the beast, by the fact that he is a killer and will eat you. In my mind that is a feature formidable and magnificent.

For myself the catching of some tiger sharks was an outstanding achievement, and that of my record tiger something never to be forgotten. The sensations this fish roused in me during the strike and battle, and especially my first sight of him, and then when he was hauled up on the sand, stand out in my memory as marvelous and indescribable.

I have written elsewhere about the wonderful setting Sydney Heads and the harbor and Sydney provide for the appreciative angler. Big sharks, big black Marlin, and his smaller cousin, the striped Marlin, will make a growing appeal to all anglers in the world who love the big rod-and-reel game, and who will take the time and spend the money to obtain it. The fact is it is not a game that can be had cheaply, although Sydney, like Avalon, California, will afford angling within the means of most sportsmen. The thing is to have them realize its greatness. Time alone can prove that. Here's to the Sydney of the future generations of anglers!

Only one thing I fear that might interfere in some

degree with my prediction. And that is¹the weather. All I saw off Sydney Heads, except for a few days, was wind. It can blow there. This, however, would only bother the overseas anglers. Australians like Bullen will fish when the weather is good. It is always irksome for anglers to come a long way and fall upon evil days, gales and rough seas. Only the persistent and passionate angler can prevail in spite of these. I do not see, however, that any really great fishing anywhere can be had without hard work, incredible patience and endurance.

During an early hour of Bowen's red-letter day with the first Marlin for Sydney Heads, I hooked a mean shark that felt like the bottom of the ocean.

It did not convince me it was a tiger, for which reason I was loath to let the boatmen pull up anchor. I fought this fish tooth and nail, and never gave it a foot of line that I could hold. All the same it kept taking yard after yard until there was a long line out. Over five hundred yards! Which is too many when there are other anchored boats around. One great feature of the Kovalovsky reel was that with five hundred yards of line out you still had a full spool left. With a long line, however, you need gradually to loosen your drag. Finally we had to up anchor and go after this mean devil.

I decided that he was a whaler shark. He worked in a manner I had learned to associate with this species. He resembled a submarine going places. But we soon caught up with him and I got most of my line back. Then I had it out with him and stopped him in a little short of an hour. Nevertheless, hauling him up to the boat was a different proposition. Peter does not often indulge in remarks at my expense, but he mildly observed that I always liked to have a fish on for a good few hours. That English crack—"a good few hours"—nettled me, although I had to laugh. Wherefore, instead of enjoying myself I settled down to grim business. I might as well have done this in the first place.

On a heavy fish deep down, the method of procedure is a short strong lift of the rod and a quick wind of the reel. You don't get in many inches each time. For a little while this is okay, but it grows to be monotonous, then tiresome, and at length painful. Of course, I had the whaler coming and he did not recover a single foot of line I gained. While I was doing this he swam inshore and obligingly returned to the neighborhood of the spot where he had made the fatal mistake of taking my bait. There, at the end of two hours and something, I heaved that whaler up to the waiting boatmen. They treated him pretty rough, I was bound to admit, and they added insult to injury by cutting a strip of meat out of him for my next bait.

This whaler was one of the bronze-backed kind, about which Dr. Stead had talked at length. It was rather rare, and a harder fighter than the black or ordinary whaler.

I could corroborate that, as it had given me as hard a fight as the eight-hundred-and-ninety-pound whaler I had caught at Bateman Bay.

Presently we were anchored again and I was fishing with a long line out and a float which buoyed my bait somewhat near the surface. Peter was boiling the billy and Love was puttering around, setting the lunch table. As I seldom ate any lunch while fishing, this procedure meant little to me, except to amuse me. I hoped to hook a fish before they sat down to tea, as I had done so many times with Peter in New Zealand. Usually we drifted while the lunch process was under way. I hooked and caught the first broadbill swordfish ever landed in New Zealand at this hour. It required several hours, to be exact, and for one monumental occasion Peter Williams forgot all about the boiling billy.

Off Sydney Heads this day my evil wishes were frustrated by fate, however, and the boys had eaten and drunk, and cleaned up their table, before I did get a strike. All of a sudden, while I was watching my bobbing cork, my daydreams were dispelled by a big gray fin cutting the water out there above my bait. But suddenly, when my cork shot under, I realized that fin belonged to a tiger shark which already had my bait. He had come up to take a look at the cork, and perhaps to bite my line. Mako often do that to floating tackle. This gray tiger, a good big one, flashed at my cork as he dragged it under. Before he could cut the line, however, I struck the hook into him hard and deep. He sheered away, plowed along the surface, then disappeared and went down deep. While he took line, Love frantically hauled up the anchor and Peter got the boat in motion.

In a few moments we were all set for battle and getting away from the other boats. I had hung, as we call it, another big fish. That for which every big-game fisherman fishes had come to pass.

During the succeeding hour and more I gave this tiger what we American fishermen slangily call the works. I whipped him thoroughly, but something happened that hindered me from completing the job. There came a queer jerky giving of my tight line, accompanied by peculiar motions of the rod tip. Usually this thing is caused by the gradual tearing of the hook from its firm hold. Many a fish I had lost after a few of these happenings.

In this case, however, nothing happened. I did not lose my fish. But the jerky slackings in my line continued, until suddenly I realized that they were caused by the shark rolling up in my leader. He would roll up a few feet, then the leader would slip or loosen, with the consequent vibrations. This was almost as bad as the tearing out of the hook. For almost any kind of a shark will roll up in the leader until he comes to the line, and then he will bite through that.

I told Peter my suspicions and he said he had arrived at

the same conclusion. "Lam into him now or you'll be losing him," he added.

A violent and persistent lamming, as Peter called it, brought that tiger shark to the surface. He came up belly first, white and wide and long, and the middle and upper part of his body was so tightly wound up in my wire leader that it cut into him. There was no coil around his gills and the last one circled his head just below his jaw. But he could open his mouth. Believe me he gaped those wide fanged jaws and shut them with the sound of a steel trap. In fact he was a trapped tiger and as mad as a hornet. He threshed his long tail and curdled the water white. But he did not appear to be able to turn over or swim. He just surged and wagged.

My swivel was scarcely two feet from those jaws. So he had thirty-three feet of wire leader wrapped around him.

"Hold hard, sir!" shouted Peter, as he leaned down with big gloved hand extended. "Just in time. A few more minutes and he'd bitten off. . . . Billy, stand by with the gaff. . . . *Wow!!!*"

When Love stuck the gaff into that shark it leaped out, half of its glistening wet body in the air, and frightfully close to the boat. The gaff did not hold. But Peter did. There was a tremendous tussle and splash. The tiger was hog-tied in my leader, but nevertheless he gave the men a bad few minutes before he was securely gaffed and roped. Even after we started to tow him ashore he kept snapping at the wire noose which had proved his un-doing.

Resting from my exertions and watching this shark while I seriously recounted the actions of gaffing and tying up to the boat, I pondered over the hazard and the difficulty of this necessary sporting procedure.

I did not blame Bullen and these other shark fisher-men for shooting sharks at close quarters out of a small boat, in some cases smaller than the shark. An attempt to gaff them would be foolhardy. I will go on record by say-ing it is better to catch a tiger shark or any great shark on a hand line, and shoot or harpoon him when he comes up to the boat, than not to catch him at all. For it is a fine thing to kill these brutes.

All the same, that is not the great, wonderful, sport-ing way to catch your big shark. The more risks you run, the harder and longer your fight with him, the stronger and finer rod and reel and line you can afford, the more creditable your achievement. There are many reasons to prove my contention, some of which I have mentioned heretofore, and one I will here repeat.

Many sharks, particularly the mako and tiger, often swim up to the boat before they are in the least whipped. In case of the mako, perhaps also the tiger, too, he comes up to see what is wrong and to do you harm. If you shoot him or harpoon him, then you destroy in one fell stroke all the commendable and manly reason for fishing for him at all, except the one of killing him.

I have never known an angler who, having once had the thrill of bringing his great fish to gaff and seeing it gaffed, ever went back to the more primitive method outlined above. Bullen himself gaffed Bowen's eight-hundred-dred-and-eighty-nine-pound tiger shark, and his boatman later gaffed a five-hundred-pound white shark. He assures me he will never shoot another. This is the nucleus of the idea I would like to inculcate in all Australian anglers. The sport is greater than they have realized. I venture to hope that the great man-eating sharks will some day have the honor accorded to lions and elephants.

CHAPTER X

BY MAY 1ST WE HAD FINISHED OUR SOUTH COAST fishing and packed to sail on the 5th for Hayman Island of the Great Barrier Reef.

Four months, at least half of which was unfishable on account of high winds and rough seas! I hesitate to state what number of fish we might have caught had we had a normal season of warm weather. But it always blows great guns when I go fishing, and otherwise handicaps me with obstacles.

Altogether we caught sixty-seven big fish, weighing over twenty-one thousand pounds, nearly ten tons. This seems incredible, but it is true, and really is nothing compared with what we might have done under favorable conditions. Two-thirds of this number fell to my rod. Bowen and his camera men, and mine, caught the rest.

My catches of a green thresher Fox shark, the first ever known to be caught, and the ninety-one-pound yellow-fin tuna, also the first ever taken in Australian waters, were surely the high lights of my good fortune. To repeat, however, no one can guess what I might have taken had the weather given us a break. Perhaps one of those giant white-death sharks! Or surely a broadbill sword-fish, that old gladiator and king of the Seven Seas.

No doubt a few words about tackle or gear in this summary will not be amiss.

I used three big tackles, favoring the Coxe, Hardy-Zane Grey and Kovalovsky reels, carrying a thousand and more yards of thirty-nine-thread Swastika lines. I really did not need fifteen hundred yards of line as I had on the big Kovalovsky, but as I was always expecting an unheard-of and monster fish, I wanted to be ready for any kind of a run.

My outfit on the camera boat had half a dozen tackles with reels not so large as mine, carrying thirty-six- and thirty-nine-thread lines. Needless to say, they ruined all these tackles, but the fun I had watching them fight fish was worth the sacrifice. I could hardly ask them to fol-low me around, running all over the ocean for four months without fishing.

For Marlin we used fifteen-foot leaders or traces, on which were mounted 13° Pflueger swordfish hooks. These traces were made out of nineteen-thread airplane cable wire and were not suitable for big sharks. We lost many leaders on hammerheads and other sharks. I had an eleven-foot mako bite one of these leaders through and escape, after leaping prodigiously.

We used hickory rods and some dualwoods made of

black palm and hickory. These were the best obtainable in the United States. I will not recommend them here because toward the end of my stay in Australia I found that Australian big-game rods are superior to ours. Bullen's Atlanta rod made by Southam is the most wonderful rod I have used. It is built of split cane in six pieces. Beyond doubt it is the most beautifully made and finished, the strongest and springiest, the most enduring rod I have ever bent upon a big fish.

The saffron-heart rod runs it a close second. As a matter of fact I am not perfectly sure which is the better. But I have not given the saffron-heart rod the same test that I gave the other.

Also it is no longer needful for Australian anglers to use American or English reels. The two new hand-made big-game-fishing reels, built for Fagan and Bullen, are just about as good as any reels I own. Upon my return to Australia I shall try out one of these.

But I have found fault with Australian traces and hooks, and especially Australian lines. These must be improved to compete with the hand-made Swastika lines.

It seems hardly necessary to say much about methods of fishing for swordfish. Most anglers have already learned that trolling with a revolving bait far back of the boat, and weighted at that, is just wasting time. Of course a starved Marlin would bite on anything; and it means little that a few fish have been caught by such methods.

Teasers trolled far back is another mistake. They should be close to the stern of the boat, around thirty feet, so that you can *see* the Marlin come, and pull them away from him.

There is no set time after the strike to hook your fish. That is something which has to do with the feel of the strike. In any event you cannot hook all of the Marlin that strike, nor catch all you hook! The great thing to learn is to find them—to run the wheels off your boat until you do find them, and that takes patience, endurance, and eyesight. I attribute my success more to the last than to anything else.

I had intended to include in this book all my data on man-eating sharks, and a chronicle of my three-and-a-half months among the islands of the Great Barrier Reef. But including photographs, this would make too large a volume. Besides, I aim to go back to the Barrier. It is a most fascinating and remarkable place—fifteen thousand square miles of waters and reefs, which have not been fished and which have incredible possibilities. I was able to identify, if not classify, three new kinds of spearfish that have never yet been taken on a rod. One is what was called a baby swordfish, from three to four feet long, which is really a matured fish. In shape it resembles a black Marlin.

A huge fifteen-foot swordfish with a short bill and broad stripes has been seen by market fishermen. And a species of sailfish, different from those I was the first to catch in the Gulf Stream, on the Pacific Coast, and in the South Seas, has been taken by market fishermen. This sailfish has a dorsal fin that is highest at the forward end and slopes back to the tail. These three fish alone will make the fame of the Barrier.

The queen fish, a beautiful silvery dolphin-like leaper, is one of the greatest fish I have caught, equal to the gallo, or rooster fish, of the Mexican coast. The mackerel that occurs in large schools is a fine light-tackle fish for anglers who do not care for the strenuous work. There is also a sea pike, a big barracuda-like fish that grows to twelve feet and more and which would be wonderful game. Undoubtedly there are more and larger fish to discover around these reefs.

The future of Australian fishing is no longer problematical.

Marlin have been sighted off Sydney Heads every month in the year. Three days before I sailed on the *Mariposa*, August 16th, a market fisherman saw five Marlin riding the swells not far offshore. In winter! A few days before that one of my men, flying down from Newcastle, saw a school of huge tiger sharks, none, he claimed, under eighteen feet, attacking a baby whale and fighting its mother. The airmen circled lower and flew round and round, not only to observe the fight, but to make sure of what was happening; and they saw the tiger sharks tear the baby whale to pieces.

Another market fisherman quite recently saw a white shark much longer than his boat, which was twenty-two feet.

Then, as I have written about before, and wish to repeat, there are a number of cases where market fishermen were towing sharks too large to pull on board, and have had these huge white devils take them in one bite. A ten- or twelve-foot shark snapped off in one bite!

A thirty-nine foot white shark was stranded at Montague Island after swallowing a small shark that had been caught on a set line. A nineteen-foot white shark was shot and harpooned off the pier at Bermagui.

Dr. David Stead, of Sydney, a scientist of international reputation, corroborates my claim that there are white sharks up to eighty feet and more. If there are not, where do the white-shark teeth, five inches across the base, come from? These have been dredged from the ocean bed.

This matter of Australian sharks is astounding. The waters around Australia are alive with many species of sharks. Why not some unknown species, huge and terrible? Who can tell what forms of life swim and battle in the ocean depths?

I predict that if I myself do not catch one of these incredible monsters, some one else will. I believe there are eighty-foot sharks. Rare, surely, but they occur! I believed in the sea serpent before the English scientist, Lieut.-Commander R. T. Gould, collected his authentic data and made the myth a fact.

It takes imagination to be a fisherman—to envision things and captures to be. Every fisherman, even if he is a skeptic and ridicules me and any supporters about these great fish, betrays himself when he goes fishing, for he goes because he imagines there are trout or salmon or Marlin, and surely a big one, waiting to strike for him. If I had not had a vivid and fertile imagination I would not have been the first to catch sailfish and swordfish in different and unfished waters of the world.

Off Freemantle large tunny have been caught by marketmen and hundreds too large to hold have broken away.

Then the West Coast of Australia! Here will be found the grandest fish. For years I have known that the Indian Ocean contains the most marvelous unfished waters, and the greatest of fish in numbers and size. I have been on the track of the monster Indian Ocean sailfish for years. But never until I met the Danish scientist, Schmidt, world authority on eels, who had seen these sailfish, did I really believe the data I had accumulated.

"Sailfish?" he repeated after me. "Oh yes indeed. I have seen them like a fleet of sailing schooners."

"And—how big?" I choked, now realizing I was on the eve of my most wonderful discovery.

"Thirty to forty feet, I should say. Their sails were easily ten feet high and fifteen feet long."

Shark's Bay, three hundred miles north of Perth, is known to contain schools of huge sharks.

Schools of sharks do not inhabit waters that are not full of fish. All the way up the West Coast to Darwin, these great fish I believe in and have been writing about have been seen.

I could fill pages with data I have collected. Some of it, most of it, is fact.

So I make my claim for Australian waters and reiterate it and will stand by it. So great is my faith that already I have enlisted the help of the Australian Government and my influential friends there, motion-picture and radio people, all of which, added to private resources and unlimited tackle, will be used to prove that Australia has fish and fishing which will dwarf all the rest known in the world today.

As for the dream and the color and the glory of such a romance, such an adventure, these are for the time being overshadowed by the immensity of the plan, and its scope, and its appalling difficulties. But these will pass and then there will come the joy of anticipation—of trolling sunny strange waters, of purple coral reefs and strips of white sand, and the shore haunts of the aboriginal—the myriads of shells, of weird birds and grand trees—and always the striving for the unattainable, whether it be a great fish or the ultimate beauty.

I have been ridiculed and criticized for claiming that Australia's thirteen thousand miles of coast would yield the greatest game fish of any waters yet discovered in the world, and all the year round.

Years ago when I predicted seven-hundred-, eight-hundred-, and thousand-pound Marlin for New Zealand, I was laughed at, even in New Zealand itself. But I and my fishing partners caught black Marlin of these weights, and established the marvelous fishing that New Zealand has enjoyed for a protracted and waning period.

After five years of correspondence with Australian scientists, missionaries, market fishermen, and sportsmen, and seven months of practical and strenuous observation and fishing, I stake my reputation that Australia will yield the most incredible and magnificent big-game fish of known and unknown species that the fishing world has ever recorded.

Added to what I just wrote about Great Barrier fish, let me append one more fact.

I have located broadbill swordfish, the genuine *Ziphias gladius,* in the shallow waters of the Gulf of Carpentaria, spawning on the white sand, as thick as fence pickets!

2. LEAPING GREEN FOX THRESHER SHARK

3. SHOWING THE PECULIAR BUILD OF THIS RARE SPECIES
ONLY ONE EVER CAPTURED

4. THE GREAT LEAPING MAKO (1)

5. THE GREAT LEAPING MAKO (II)

6. THE GREAT LEAPING MAKO (III)

7. THE GREAT LEAPING MAKO (IV)

8. AUSTRALIAN-RECORD BLACK MARLIN, 480 POUNDS

9. AUSTRALIAN BLACK MARLIN, 403 POUNDS

10. YELLOW-FIN TUNA. FIRST TO BE REPORTED ON AUSTRALIAN COAST
VERY VALUABLE COMMERCIAL DISCOVERY

11. THE WANDERING ALBATROSS

12. 805-POUND TIGER SHARK

13. GAFFING A GRAY NURSE SHARK

14. GRAY NURSE UNDER WATER

15. ONE DAY'S CATCH OF GRAY NURSE SHARKS, 350 TO 500 POUNDS

16. Z. G. ON THE ROD

17. THE WOBBEGONG, OR CARPET SHARK
NOTE FILAMENTS OF SKIN PROTRUDING FROM LIPS
THESE HE USES TO LURE SMALL FISH

18 THE "AVALON," CAMPWARD BOUND, FLYING FLAGS

19. TIGER SHARK WRAPPED IN THE LEADER

20. HOLDING HARD ON A VANQUISHED MARLIN

21. THE "UNDOYOU"

22. WHALER SHARK, 890 POUNDS. A VICIOUS MAN-EATER THAT GOES UP THE RIVERS

23. Z. G. CAMP AT BATEMANS' BAY

24. LEAPING STRIPED MARLIN (1)

25. LEAPING STRIPED MARLIN (II)

26. LEAPING STRIPED MARLIN (III)

27. LEAPING STRIPED MARLIN (IV)

28. LEAPING STRIPED MARLIN (V)

29. LEAPING STRIPED MARLIN (VI)

30. LEAPING STRIPED MARLIN (VII)

31. LEAPING STRIPED MARLIN (VIII)

32. AUSTRALIAN-RECORD STRIPED MARLIN, 324 POUNDS (IX)

33. ONE DAY'S CATCH, AVERAGING 278 POUNDS (X)

34. WHITE DEATH SHARK
SHOWING RESEMBLANCE IN SHAPE TO THE BROADBILL SWORDFISH

35. SHOWING JAWS AND TEETH OF THE TERRIBLE WHITE DEATH SHARK, FIERCEST AND DEADLIEST OF ALL MAN-EATERS